PUBLISHER'S NOTE

V&S Publishers has carved a significant niche in the publishing industry over the last decade, having successfully published more than 1000 titles across 9 languages spanning over 50 subject categories. Being known for the quality of content, we have built a reputation of excellence and reliability. We have consistently delivered **"Value & Substance"** to our readers, through a wide range of titles across a variety of genres covering school books, fiction and non-fiction that caters to different people from every section of the society.

The **Olympiad Guidebooks for classes 1-10** across all subjects, launched almost a decade ago, under the **GEN X Imprint**, became a go-to-source for the school students in no time, owing to their invaluable and substantive content written in a guidebook pattern,.

Having successfully sold a million copies of the same and in response to demand by both students as well as shopkeepers nationwide; we now present before you our newly launched **Olympiad Workbook Series**, designed for **classes 1-10 across 4 subjects**.

The workbooks are meticulously curated by a team of experienced educators, researchers and subject matter experts, edited by professionals and peer reviewed by teachers. The team has poured its efforts and expertise into creating a crisp and concise workbook which will help and guide the students to the path of success in Olympiad exams. The **MCQs** identified will not only help in scoring top marks in Olympiads but also inculcate a sense of deeper understanding of the subject, by way of solving **HOTS** and referring to complete solutions at the end of the book.

Here we present our new release– **OLYMPIAD WORKBOOK (NSO) CLASS–8** having following features:

☞ Based on the latest syllabi
☞ MCQs with comprehensive coverage of topics
☞ HOTS Questions liberally included
☞ A dedicated chapter on logical reasoning
☞ Model test paper for thorough practice
☞ Sample OMR sheet for real time simulation

We have made sure through our best efforts, that this workbook strictly follows the latest syllabi and patterns of the Olympiad Examination.

As **V&S Publishers** continuously strive to enhance the readability and maintain the credibility of our academic publications, we seek the support of our valuable readers in influencing and enriching the lives of future generations of students.

P.S. While every care has been taken to ensure the correctness of the content, if you come across any error, howsoever minor, do not hesitate to discuss with teachers while pointing that out to us in no uncertain terms.

We wish you all the best for your exams!

DISTINCTIVE FEATURES

01

Learning Objectives

They list the whole chapter as subtopics, helping the teachers to guide children in a step-by-step manner.

02

Multiple Choice Questions

MCQs act as an excellent learning aid, helping you to understand and work on your mistakes.

03

HOTS (Achievers Section)

The High Order Thinking Questions aim to help the student to solve Application-based questions and gain practical understanding of the subject.

Model Test Paper

Model test paper are provided at the end of each book, which help the student to test the knowledge which they have gained after thorough reading of all chapters.

04

Answer Key

Detailed Answer Key along with explanations aid the pupil to indentify, understand the mistakes they make during the course of Olympiad preparation.

05

OLYMPIAD WORKBOOK

8

NATIONAL SCIENCE OLYMPIAD

- **01** Learning Objectives
- **02** Multiple Choice Questions
- **03** HOTS (Achievers Section)
- **04** Model Test Paper
- **05** Answer Keys and Solutions
- **06** OMR Answer Sheet

V&S PUBLISHERS

Published by:

V&S PUBLISHERS

F-2/16, Ansari road, Daryaganj, New Delhi-110002
☎ 23240026, 23240027 • *Fax:* 011-23240028
✉ info@vspublishers.com • ⊕ www.vspublishers.com

 **Online Brandstore: amazon.in/vspublishers**

Regional Office : Hyderabad
5-1-707/1, Brij Bhawan (Beside Central Bank of India Lane)
Bank Street, Koti, Hyderabad - 500 095
☎ 040-24737290
✉ vspublishershyd@gmail.com

Follow us on:   

BUY OUR BOOKS FROM: AMAZON   FLIPKART

© Copyright: *V&S* PUBLISHERS
ISBN 978-81-977761-7-5
New Edition

CONTENTS

CROP PRODUCTION AND MANAGEMENT

LEARNING OBJECTIVES

- ➤ Various agricultural practices
- ➤ Basic practices of crop production
- ➤ The process of sowing of seeds
- ➤ The importance of preparation of soil
- ➤ Animal husbandry

MULTIPLE CHOICE QUESTIONS

1. Which of these is not a kharif crop?
   (A) rice (B) maize
   (C) wheat (D) ground nut

2. Anil added some material from the packets to the beakers containing moist soil and gram seeds. Only the seeds of one beaker showed fast growth. The material added is ________.
   (A) fertilizer (B) manure
   (C) soil (D) water

3. Ploughing is done for ________.
   (A) harvesting
   (B) preparation
   (C) weeding
   (D) irrigation

4. Which one of these is not a type of fertilizer?
   (A) nitrogenous fertilizer
   (B) phosphate fertilizer
   (C) potassium fertilizer
   (D) none of these

5. What is the full form of FYM?
   (A) Farm yield manure
   (B) Foreign yard manure
   (C) Farm yard manure
   (D) Full yield manure

6. Which crop is cultivated by transplantation method of sowing?
   (A) paddy (B) wheat
   (C) maize (D) barley

7. ________ crops are the plants that are grown for producing products that are the sources of income for an economy.
   (A) Food (B) Cash
   (C) Ragi (D) Kharif

8. Which one of these is a cash crop?
   (A) Sugarcane (B) Oil seeds
   (C) Jute fibre (D) All of these

9. Tomatoes are cultivated by the practice called ________.
   (A) Transpiration
   (B) Translocation
   (C) Transportation
   (D) Transplantation

10. The crops grown in India in rainy season are called ________.
    (A) Rabi crops
    (B) Kharif crops
    (C) Zaid crops
    (D) Cash crops

11. The crops that are grown in India in winter and summer season are alled _________.
   (A) Zaid crops   (B) Rabi crops
   (C) Kharif crops   (D) Cash crops

12. The crops that are grown in India in summer season are called _________.
   (A) Zaid crops   (B) Hot crops
   (C) Rabi crops   (D) Kharif crops

13. Which one of these does not belong to group?
   (A) Weed   (B) Insect
   (C) Urea   (D) Fungus

14. Which of these is not a fungal disease of plants?
   (A) Rust   (B) Wilt
   (C) Smut   (D) Blight

15. Which of the flouring machines can be used to harvest a crop and also to beat out the grain from the chaff?
   (A) Harvester
   (B) Combine
   (C) Thresher
   (D) Harrow

16. Which of these is not true about ploughing?
   (A) It loosens the soil.
   (B) It prevents soil erosion.
   (C) It aerates the soil.
   (D) It allows easy penetration of roots into the soil.

17. Separation of healthy seeds of wheat from unhealthy seeds can be done by _________.
   (A) water
   (B) using threshing
   (C) putting seeds in water
   (D) winnowing

18. When seeds of wheat are pat in water, the healthy seeds will _________.
   (A) sink to the bottom
   (B) float on the top
   (C) float in centre
   (D) none of these

19. The two crops which are not grown by sowing their seeds directly into the soil in large fields are _________.
   (i)   Peas   (ii) Tomatoes
   (iii) Chillies   (iv) Maize
   (A) i & ii   (B) ii & iii
   (C) i & iii   (D) Only iii

20. The unwanted plants that grow along with the main crop in the field are called _________.
   (A) Cereal   (B) Tiny creeds
   (C) Weedicides   (D) Weeds

21. Compost lacks in which of the following nutrients?
   (A) Nitrogen
   (B) Phosphorous
   (C) Potassium
   (D) All of these

22. Compost is rich in _________.
   (A) Organic compounds
   (B) Nitrogen
   (C) Potash
   (D) Urea

23. A traditional method of sowing by scattering is called _________.
   (A) Spreading
   (B) Broadcasting
   (C) Telecasting
   (D) Threshing

24. Separation of grains from chaff is the process called _________.
   (A) Broadcasting
   (B) Threshing
   (C) Winnowing
   (D) separation

25. Ammonium phosphate is a fertilizer of which type?
   (A) Nitrogenous fertilizer
   (B) Phosphatic fertilizer
   (C) Potassic fertilizer
   (D) Organic fertilizer

26. The branch of science that deals with growing plants and raising livestock for human use is
    (A) Agriculture
    (B) Horticulture
    (C) Pisciculture
    (D) Animal husbandry

27. Products obtained from the crops are called
    (A) Yield
    (B) Produce
    (C) Crop
    (D) Fertilisers

28. The practice of growing two or more dissimilar crops in the same field one after another is
    (A) Crop rotation
    (B) Tilling
    (C) Plantation
    (D) Weeding

29. Which of the following pairs are incorrectly matched?
    (A) Growing flowers - Horticulture
    (B) Growing food corps - Agriculture
    (C) Bee keeping - Sericulture
    (D) Cultivating grapes - Viticulture

30. The ideal months for harvesting kharif crop are
    (A) June/July
    (B) August/September
    (C) September/October
    (D) November/December

─Darken Your Choice with HB Pencil─

1.	Ⓐ Ⓑ Ⓒ Ⓓ	7.	Ⓐ Ⓑ Ⓒ Ⓓ	13.	Ⓐ Ⓑ Ⓒ Ⓓ	19	Ⓐ Ⓑ Ⓒ Ⓓ	25.	Ⓐ Ⓑ Ⓒ Ⓓ
2.	Ⓐ Ⓑ Ⓒ Ⓓ	8.	Ⓐ Ⓑ Ⓒ Ⓓ	14.	Ⓐ Ⓑ Ⓒ Ⓓ	20.	Ⓐ Ⓑ Ⓒ Ⓓ	26.	Ⓐ Ⓑ Ⓒ Ⓓ
3.	Ⓐ Ⓑ Ⓒ Ⓓ	9.	Ⓐ Ⓑ Ⓒ Ⓓ	15.	Ⓐ Ⓑ Ⓒ Ⓓ	21.	Ⓐ Ⓑ Ⓒ Ⓓ	27.	Ⓐ Ⓑ Ⓒ Ⓓ
4.	Ⓐ Ⓑ Ⓒ Ⓓ	10.	Ⓐ Ⓑ Ⓒ Ⓓ	16.	Ⓐ Ⓑ Ⓒ Ⓓ	22.	Ⓐ Ⓑ Ⓒ Ⓓ	28.	Ⓐ Ⓑ Ⓒ Ⓓ
5.	Ⓐ Ⓑ Ⓒ Ⓓ	11.	Ⓐ Ⓑ Ⓒ Ⓓ	17.	Ⓐ Ⓑ Ⓒ Ⓓ	23.	Ⓐ Ⓑ Ⓒ Ⓓ	29.	Ⓐ Ⓑ Ⓒ Ⓓ
6.	Ⓐ Ⓑ Ⓒ Ⓓ	12.	Ⓐ Ⓑ Ⓒ Ⓓ	18.	Ⓐ Ⓑ Ⓒ Ⓓ	24.	Ⓐ Ⓑ Ⓒ Ⓓ	30.	Ⓐ Ⓑ Ⓒ Ⓓ

MICROORGANISMS

LEARNING OBJECTIVES

➤ Basic structure of bacteria, fungi, algae and protozoa
➤ Beneficial and harmful effects of micro-organisms
➤ The complete process of nitrogen- fixation

MULTIPLE CHOICE QUESTIONS

1. Microorganisms can be grouped as ________.
   (A) Bacteria and fungi
   (B) Viruses
   (C) Algae and protozoa
   (D) All of these

2. Which of the following cannot be classified as either living or non-living micro-organism?
   (A) Fungi   (B) Viruses
   (C) Bacteria   (D) Protozoa

3. Which of these is not a fungus?
   (A) Virus   (B) Yeast
   (C) Mushroom   (D) Mould

4. Which of the following make their own food by photosynthesis?
   (A) Virus   (B) Bacteria
   (C) Algae   (D) Protozoa

5. Spongyness of bread is because of ________.
   (A) Bread mould
   (B) Orange mould
   (C) Freshness
   (D) None of these

6. Which of the following is responsible for making bread soft and lighter?
   (A) Sugar and salt
   (B) Finely grounded
   (C) CO_2 gas given off during fermentation of sugar
   (D) Alcohol released during fermentation of sugar

7. In food preservation process, the technique used is /are ________.
   (A) Killing the microbes
   (B) Making them inactive
   (C) Both (A) and (B)
   (D) None of these

8. Which of these micro-organisms do not have a regular cell structure?
   (A) Viruses   (B) Bacteria
   (C) Protozoa   (D) Algae

9. A drop of greenish pond water seen under a microscope has ________.
   (A) green colour creatures
   (B) green water colour
   (C) microorganisms
   (D) none of these

10. Which of these are found as both unicellular and multicellular?
    (A) Bacteria   (B) Algae
    (C) Viruses   (D) Moulds

11. The bacterium found in curd is called ________.

(A) *Lactobacillus*
(B) *Bacillus*
(C) *Acetobacter*
(D) *Salmonella typhi*

12. Micro-organisms spread though ________.
(A) air
(B) water
(C) curd
(D) all of these

13. What in the shape of *Lactobacillus*, the bacterium used for making cheese and curd?
(A) Curved
(B) oval
(C) Cylindrical
(D) spiral

14. A lukewarm sugar solution of yeast when seen under a microscope after a day shows that ________.
(A) Sugar is present
(B) Yeast cell is present
(C) Bacteria are present
(D) A chain of yeast cells are present

15. A chain of yeast cells in a warm sugar solution means ________.
(A) Yeast cells are reproduced by budding
(B) Yeast cells got multiplied
(C) Yeast cells form a chain
(D) None of these

16. Microorganisms are classified into how many classes?
(A) 3
(B) 4
(C) 5
(D) 6

17. Which of the following increases the fertility of soil?
(A) Vermicompost
(B) Manure
(C) Industrial waste
(D) Both (A) and (B)

18. Protozoans are unicellular ______ organisms.
(i) Lactobacillus bacteria
(ii) Rhizobium bacteria
(iii) Spirogyra algae
(iv) Blue – green algae
(A) (i) & (ii)
(B) (ii) & (iii)
(C) (i) & (iv)
(D) (ii) & (iv)

19. The softening of dough mixed with yeast is called ________.
(A) baking process
(B) transformation
(C) fermentation
(D) distillation

20. Orange mould is a fungus found growing on decaying ________.
(A) Citrus fruit
(B) Malta
(C) Orange
(D) All of these

21. Vinegar is made from which of these bacteria?
(A) A centobacteraceti
(B) Pseudomonas putida
(C) Lactobacillus
(D) None of these

22. Which of these diseases is caused by Plasmodium?
(A) Tuberculosis
(B) Typhoid
(C) Malaria
(D) Headache

23. Dead or weakened germs that help protect the body against future attack by the germs are called ________.
(A) Antibiotics
(B) Vaccine
(C) Medicine
(D) None of these

24. Amoeba, guardian paramecium are examples of ________.
(A) Bacterium
(B) Virus
(C) Protozoan
(D) Fungi

25. Microorganisms are useful in ________.
(A) Food and beverage industry
(B) Making medicines and vaccines
(C) Cleaning the environment
(D) All of these

26. Tiny organisms which cannot be seen with the naked eyes are called
    (A) microorganisms
    (B) animals
    (C) fungi
    (D) bacteria

27. Microorganisms are also known as
    (A) yeast
    (B) microbes
    (C) viruses
    (D) Amoeba

28. Fungus can be seen with a
    (A) microscope
    (B) telescope
    (C) magnifying glass
    (D) both (A) and (C)

29. Microorganisms that causes disease are also known as
    (A) pathogens
    (B) fungi
    (C) antigen
    (D) microbes

30. Pathogens are also called
    (A) germs
    (B) antigen
    (C) antibody
    (D) carrier

1.	Ⓐ Ⓑ Ⓒ Ⓓ	7.	Ⓐ Ⓑ Ⓒ Ⓓ	13.	Ⓐ Ⓑ Ⓒ Ⓓ	19	Ⓐ Ⓑ Ⓒ Ⓓ	25.	Ⓐ Ⓑ Ⓒ Ⓓ
2.	Ⓐ Ⓑ Ⓒ Ⓓ	8.	Ⓐ Ⓑ Ⓒ Ⓓ	14.	Ⓐ Ⓑ Ⓒ Ⓓ	20.	Ⓐ Ⓑ Ⓒ Ⓓ	26.	Ⓐ Ⓑ Ⓒ Ⓓ
3.	Ⓐ Ⓑ Ⓒ Ⓓ	9.	Ⓐ Ⓑ Ⓒ Ⓓ	15.	Ⓐ Ⓑ Ⓒ Ⓓ	21.	Ⓐ Ⓑ Ⓒ Ⓓ	27.	Ⓐ Ⓑ Ⓒ Ⓓ
4.	Ⓐ Ⓑ Ⓒ Ⓓ	10.	Ⓐ Ⓑ Ⓒ Ⓓ	16.	Ⓐ Ⓑ Ⓒ Ⓓ	22.	Ⓐ Ⓑ Ⓒ Ⓓ	28.	Ⓐ Ⓑ Ⓒ Ⓓ
5.	Ⓐ Ⓑ Ⓒ Ⓓ	11.	Ⓐ Ⓑ Ⓒ Ⓓ	17.	Ⓐ Ⓑ Ⓒ Ⓓ	23.	Ⓐ Ⓑ Ⓒ Ⓓ	29.	Ⓐ Ⓑ Ⓒ Ⓓ
6.	Ⓐ Ⓑ Ⓒ Ⓓ	12.	Ⓐ Ⓑ Ⓒ Ⓓ	18.	Ⓐ Ⓑ Ⓒ Ⓓ	24.	Ⓐ Ⓑ Ⓒ Ⓓ	30.	Ⓐ Ⓑ Ⓒ Ⓓ

SYNTHETIC FIBRES AND PLASTICS

LEARNING OBJECTIVES

➤ Properties of natural and synthetic polymers
➤ The characteristics of synthetic fibres
➤ Different properties of rayon, nylon, polyester

MULTIPLE CHOICE QUESTIONS

1. Which of these is a natural fibre?
   (A) Polyester
   (B) Cotton
   (C) Rayon
   (D) Nylon

2. Regarding nylon, which of the following options is correct?
   (A) Protein
   (B) Polyester
   (C) Polyamide
   (D) Cellulose

3. Terylene, Terene and Dacron are different types of which fibre?
   (A) Polyester
   (B) Rayon
   (C) Nylon
   (D) None of these

4. Which of these fibers is derived from chemicals?
   (A) Rayon
   (B) Cotton
   (C) Nylon
   (D) Silk

5. Which of these fibers is made from wood?
   (A) Rayon
   (B) Nylon
   (C) Terylene
   (D) Cotton

6. Rayon is prepared by _________.
   (A) Solvay's
   (B) Haber's process
   (C) Electrolysis
   (D) Viscose process

7. Polythene is a polymer which is used to make _________.
   (A) Tyres
   (B) Shoes
   (C) Plastic containers
   (D) Textiles

8. Nylon is used in making of _________.
   (A) Conveyor belts
   (B) Fishing nets
   (C) Combs
   (D) Toothbrush bristles

9. Human-made fibres made from polymers are _________.
   (A) Monomers
   (B) Synthetic fibres
   (C) Plastic fibres
   (D) Artificial fibres

10. Which of these is a thermosetting plastic?
    (A) Polystyrene
    (B) Polythene
    (C) Bakelite
    (D) PVC

11. Which of them is a polymer?
    (A) Bakelite
    (B) Polystyrene
    (C) Polythene
    (D) All of these

12. A substance becomes soft on heating and can be moulded into different shapes. It is called __________.
   (A) Rubber
   (B) Nylon
   (C) Rayon
   (D) Polythene

13. Monomers are the basic unit of __________.
   (A) Polymers
   (B) Chemicals
   (C) Bad conductor of electricity
   (D) Inflammable

14. Which one of the following is a fireproof plastic?
   (A) Bad conductor of heat
   (B) Water soluble
   (C) Bad conductor of electricity
   (D) Inflammable

15. Which one of the following cannot catch fire?
   (A) Melamine
   (B) Bakelite
   (C) Polythene
   (D) Teflon

16. Which of these can be used as a substitute for glass of windows in cars?
   (A) Fibre optic
   (B) Glass fibre
   (C) Teflon
   (D) Perspex

17. On the basis of activity, the strongest fibre is __________.
   (A) Nylon
   (B) Polyester
   (C) Silk
   (D) Rayon

18. Which of the following is a monomer of polythene?
   (A) Chlorine
   (B) Methane
   (C) Ethylene
   (D) Iodine

19. Which fibre is called artificial silk?
   (A) Rayon
   (B) Nylon
   (C) Polyester
   (D) Acrylic

20. PVC stands for __________.
   (A) Plastic very common in use
   (B) Plastic vinyl chloride
   (C) Poly vinyl chloride
   (D) Polymer vinyl chloride

21. A paper strip is immersed in NaOH and then in carbon disulphide (CS_2). The liquid obtained is __________.
   (A) Nylon   (B) Viscose
   (C) Plastic   (D) Cellulose

22. NaOH and __________ are solutions used in the preparation of rayon.
   (A) H_2SO_4 (B) HCl
   (C) CO_2 (D) $C_{12}O_6H_{12}$

23. Which fibre is used in making of conveyor belts?
   (A) Polyester   (B) Rayon
   (C) Nylon   (D) Acrylic

24. Which type of plastic cannot be reheated again to form new shapes?
   (A) Thermoplastic
   (B) Thermosetting
   (C) Both (A) and (B)
   (D) Nylon

25. Which substance is used in coating for making non-sticky utensils?
   (A) Formica   (B) Melamine
   (C) Teflon   (D) Perspex

26. The process of taking out threads from the silk cocoon is called _________.
    (A) rearing
    (B) searing
    (C) scouring
    (D) reeling

27. Which of the following products cannot be decomposed easily?
    (A) Acrylic
    (B) Plastic
    (C) Polyethene
    (D) All of these

28. Which of the following statements is not true?
    (A) Polymer occurs in nature.
    (B) Cotton thread is stronger than nylon thread.
    (C) Cellulose is made of glucose units.
    (D) Nylon is used to make parachute.

29. Which of the following is a characteristic of plastics?
    (A) Electrical conductors
    (B) Heat conductors
    (C) Biodegradable
    (D) Non-biodegradable

30. Plastics that retain their plasticity on repeated heating are called
    (A) thermosetting plastics
    (B) thermoplastics
    (C) thermal plastics
    (D) none of these

Darken Your Choice with HB Pencil

1.	(A) (B) (C) (D)	7.	(A) (B) (C) (D)	13.	(A) (B) (C) (D)	19	(A) (B) (C) (D)	25.	(A) (B) (C) (D)
2.	(A) (B) (C) (D)	8.	(A) (B) (C) (D)	14.	(A) (B) (C) (D)	20.	(A) (B) (C) (D)	26.	(A) (B) (C) (D)
3.	(A) (B) (C) (D)	9.	(A) (B) (C) (D)	15.	(A) (B) (C) (D)	21.	(A) (B) (C) (D)	27.	(A) (B) (C) (D)
4.	(A) (B) (C) (D)	10.	(A) (B) (C) (D)	16.	(A) (B) (C) (D)	22.	(A) (B) (C) (D)	28.	(A) (B) (C) (D)
5.	(A) (B) (C) (D)	11.	(A) (B) (C) (D)	17.	(A) (B) (C) (D)	23.	(A) (B) (C) (D)	29.	(A) (B) (C) (D)
6.	(A) (B) (C) (D)	12.	(A) (B) (C) (D)	18.	(A) (B) (C) (D)	24.	(A) (B) (C) (D)	30.	(A) (B) (C) (D)

METALS AND NON-METALS

LEARNING OBJECTIVES

➤ The classification of metals and non-metals
➤ Different chemical reactions of metals
➤ Different types of chemical reactions with non-metals

MULTIPLE CHOICE QUESTIONS

1. A metal which exists in liquid state ________.
   (A) Gallium
   (B) Mercury
   (C) Sodium
   (D) Potassium
2. Which of the following property regarding metal is correct?
   (A) Low melting and boiling point
   (B) High melting and boiling point
   (C) Low melting and high boiling point
   (D) High melting and low boiling point
3. Choose the correct one for metal.
   (A) Brittle and ductile
   (B) Malleable and ductile
   (C) Non-malleable and ductile
   (D) Non-malleable
4. A substance composed of two or more metals is called ________.
   (A) Metalloids
   (B) Non-metals
   (C) Alloys
   (D) All of these
5. Which one of the following is a metal?
   (A) Gold
   (B) Silver
   (C) Aluminum
   (D) All of these
6. Which one of the following is a non-metal?
   (A) Copper
   (B) Chlorine
   (C) Hydrogen
   (D) Both (B) and (C)

7. Metals generally forms ________.
   (A) Basic oxides
   (B) Acidic oxides
   (C) Neutral oxides
   (D) None of these
8. A metal which melts on the palm ________.
   (A) Zinc
   (B) Gallium
   (C) Sodium
   (D) Potassium
9. A metal which is a poor conductor of heat ________.
   (A) Zinc
   (B) Gold
   (C) Iron
   (D) Lead
10. The most abundant element in the universe is ________.
    (A) Hydrogen
    (B) Oxygen
    (C) Silicon
    (D) Helium
11. The most abundant metal on the earth is ________.
    (A) Aluminium
    (B) Gold
    (C) Copper
    (D) Iron
12. A lustrous non-metal is ________.
    (A) Sulphur
    (B) Iodine
    (C) Diamond
    (D) Phosphorus
13. Metals are ________.
    (A) Semi conductor of heat and electricity
    (B) Good conductor of heat and electricity
    (C) Bad conductor of heat and electricity
    (D) Good conductor of heat but bad conductor of electricity

14. Which of the following is a basic oxide?
(A) CaO   (B) CO_2
(C) H_2O (D) N_2O

15. Metals can be drawn into thin wires, this property of metal is known as ________.
(A) Conductivity   (B) Ductility
(C) Malleability   (D) Both (B) and (C)

16. The property due to which non-metals break on hammering is called ________.
(A) Ductility   (B) Malleability
(C) Brittleness   (D) Conductivity

17. The tip of lead pencil is made of ________.
(A) Lead   (B) Zinc
(C) Charcoal   (D) Graphite

18. Iron burns in air to form ________.
(A) FeO   (B) FeO_2
(C) Fe_2O_3 (D) Fe_3O_4

19. Arrange the following metal in increasing order of their reactivity towards water: Zinc, Iron, Magnesium, Sodium.
(A) Iron < Zinc < Magnesium < Sodium
(B) Iron < Magnesium < Sodium < Zinc
(C) Magnesium < Iron < Sodium < Zinc
(D) Sodium < Iron < Magnesium < Zinc

20. Which of the following statement(s) are not correct?
Statement 1: All Metals are malleable and ductile
Statement 2: Non-metals are non-malleable and ductile
(A) Statement 1
(B) Statement 2
(C) Both are correct
(D) Both are incorrect

21. Which one of the following statements are correct?
Statement 1: Metals are lustrous
Statement 2: Non-metals are not lustrous
(A) Statement 1
(B) Statement 2
(C) Both statements are correct
(D) Both statements are incorrect

22. What will happen if copper wire is dipped in iron (II) sulphate solution?
(A) Copper sulphate is formed
(B) Copper is formed
(C) Iron is formed
(D) No reaction

23. What is the nature of the oxides which formed when a metal reacts with oxygen?
(A) Acidic   (B) Basic
(C) Neutral   (D) None of these

24. What is the nature of the oxide which is formed when a non-metal reacts with oxygen?
(A) Acidic   (B) Basic
(C) Neutral   (D) None of these

25. Which non-metal is used as electrodes in electrolytic cells and dry cells?
(A) Diamond   (B) Phosphorus
(C) Graphite   (D) Hydrogen

26. Acidic solution turns ________.
(A) Red litmus blue
(B) Blue litmus red
(C) Red litmus green
(D) No reaction

27. Basic solution turns ________.
(A) Red litmus blue
(B) Red litmus green
(C) Blue litmus red
(D) No reacting

28. Which metal is used in the thermometers and barometers?
(A) Mercury   (B) Iron
(C) Silver   (D) Gold

29. Sodium is a ________.
(A) Colourless and hard metal
(B) Silvery white and very soft metal
(C) Silvery white and hard metal
(D) Colourless and soft metal

30. Which non-metal is the hardest substance known?
(A) Graphite   (B) Phosphorus
(C) Diamond   (D) Hydrogen

31. Given below are some physical properties of metals. Which of the following is not true?

    i.   Metals in the pure state possess lusture.
    ii. Metals have low tensile strength.
    iii. Metals are non-sonorous.

    (A) Only i   (B) Only ii
    (C) i and ii   (D) ii and iii

32. Which is the hardest substance?
    (A) Gold   (B) Diamond
    (C) Aluminium   (D) None of these

33. Metals react with acids to produce respective salts with evolution of
    (A) hydrogen gas   (B) oxygen gas
    (C) CO_2 gas   (D) none of these

34. In displacement reactions
    (A) a more reactive metal displaces a less reactive metal.
    (B) a less reactive metal displaces a more reactive metal.
    (C) both (A) and (B)
    (D) none of these

35. Which of the following non-metals are used in fertilisers?
    (A) Nitrogen
    (B) Phosphorus
    (C) Both (A) and (B)
    (D) None of these

Darken Your Choice with HB Pencil

1.	A B C D	8.	A B C D	15.	A B C D	22	A B C D	29.	A B C D
2.	A B C D	9.	A B C D	16.	A B C D	23.	A B C D	30.	A B C D
3.	A B C D	10.	A B C D	17.	A B C D	24.	A B C D	31.	A B C D
4.	A B C D	11.	A B C D	18.	A B C D	25.	A B C D	32.	A B C D
5.	A B C D	12.	A B C D	19.	A B C D	26.	A B C D	33.	A B C D
6.	A B C D	13.	A B C D	20.	A B C D	27.	A B C D	34.	A B C D
7.	A B C D	14.	A B C D	21.	A B C D	28.	A B C D	35.	A B C D

COAL AND PETROLEUM

LEARNING OBJECTIVES

➤ The importance of natural resources
➤ The formation and composition of petroleum
➤ Natural and compressed natural gases

MULTIPLE CHOICE QUESTIONS

1. Renewable resources need to be conserved because ________.
   (A) they are slowly getting exhausted.
   (B) we are using them faster than they are replenished by nature.
   (C) if we overuse them, nature will stop replacing them.
   (D) all of these

2. A substrata which produces sufficient energy on burning is called ________.
   (A) biogas
   (B) oxidising agent
   (C) fuel
   (D) combustion mass

3. Which of these is an important fraction of petroleum and is farther distilled to get lubricating oil and paraffin wax.
   (A) petroleum
   (B) heavy oil
   (C) anthracite
   (D) residue

4. The resources that either never run out, or those that are replaced within a reasonable period of time through natural processes are called as ________.
   (A) renewable resources
   (B) non-renewable resources
   (C) exhaustible resources
   (D) replenishable resources

5. Which of these is not a renewable resource?
   (A) air
   (B) sunlight
   (C) water
   (D) petroleum

6. Destructive distillation of coal produces ________.
   (A) petrol
   (B) paraffin wax
   (C) coal gas
   (D) diesel

7. The best quality of coal is ________.
   (A) peat
   (B) anthracite
   (C) lignite
   (D) bituminous

8. Which of the following is a non-polluting fuel for vehicles?
   (A) petrol
   (B) diesel
   (C) kerosene
   (D) CNG

9. Which energy is contained in fuels that is locked within the chemical bonds of their constituent molecules?
   (A) potential energy
   (B) kinetic energy
   (C) heat energy
   (D) light energy

10. A fossil fuel is ________.
    (A) coal
    (B) petroleum
    (C) natural gas
    (D) all of these

11. Which type of coal is used for household purposes?
(A) peat (B) bituminous
(C) lignite (D) anthracite

12. In destructive distillation coal is heated strongly to about _______.
(A) 500°C (B) 100°C
(C) 1000°C (D) 3000°C

13. Petroleum and natural gas were formed from _______.
(A) dead sea animals
(B) dead trees
(C) dead weeds and small plants
(D) heat produced in the sea bed

14. Which of these is not a natural source of energy?
(A) coal (B) electricity
(C) petroleum (D) sun

15. As coal contains mainly carbon, the slow process of conversion of buried vegetation into coal is called _______.
(A) carbonisation
(B) distillation
(C) ionisation
(D) fossilisation

16. The two places in India famous for their oil wells are _______.
(A) Bihar and MP
(B) Assam and Maharashtra
(C) Bihar and Assam
(D) Rajasthan and Maharashtra

17. Fuels which are obtained from nature are called _______.
(A) primary fuels
(B) natural fuels
(C) exhaustible fuels
(D) inexhaustible fuels

18. Natural gas mainly contains _______.
(A) ethane
(B) hydrogen
(C) nitrogen
(D) methane

19. Bituminous coal has about _______ carbon.
(A) 92% (B) 65%
(C) 38% (D) 75%

20. Which of these is not a fossil fuel?
(A) CNG (B) LPG
(C) Petrol (D) Hydrogen

21. Fractional distillation of petroleum is done at _______.
(A) 100°C (B) 400°C
(C) 500°C (D) 700°C

22. Which of these is obtained by destructive distillation of coal?
(A) LPG (B) CNG
(C) Coal gas (D) Methane

23. Ammonical liquor is collected during the destructive distillation of coal in _______.
(A) decliner tube
(B) as a precipitate
(C) boiling tube
(D) test–tube with water

24. The process of separating a mixture of two or more liquids having different boiling points by collecting their vapours art controlled temperature is called _______.
(A) refining
(B) fractional distillation
(C) destructive distilation
(D) none of these

25. The residue left behind when destructive distillation of coal is carried out is _______.
(A) coal gas
(B) coke
(C) coal tar
(D) Ammonium compound

26. An ideal fuel:
    i.   should burn at a moderate rate.
    ii. should not produce any poisonous and irritating fumes during burning.
    iii. should leave residue after burning.
    Which of the options goes with in line given in the question?
    (A) Only i
    (B) Only ii
    (C) Both i and ii
    (D) Both ii and iii

27. What should be the characteristic of rocket fuel?
    (A) Light and compact
    (B) High calorific value
    (C) Should burn rapidly
    (D) All of these

28. A family consumes 12 Kg of LPG in 30 days. Calculate the average energy consumed per day if the calorific value of LPG is 50 K J/Kg.
    (A) 20,000 J/day
    (B) 10,000 J/day
    (C) 15,000 J/day
    (D) 25,000 J/day

29. The mining of oil under sea is termed as
    (A) distillation
    (B) carbonisation
    (C) shore mining
    (D) destructive distillation

30. Petroleum is separated by using the difference in
    (A) ignition temperatures
    (B) melting points
    (C) freezing points
    (D) boiling points

Darken Your Choice with HB Pencil

1.	Ⓐ Ⓑ Ⓒ Ⓓ	7.	Ⓐ Ⓑ Ⓒ Ⓓ	13.	Ⓐ Ⓑ Ⓒ Ⓓ	19	Ⓐ Ⓑ Ⓒ Ⓓ	25.	Ⓐ Ⓑ Ⓒ Ⓓ
2.	Ⓐ Ⓑ Ⓒ Ⓓ	8.	Ⓐ Ⓑ Ⓒ Ⓓ	14.	Ⓐ Ⓑ Ⓒ Ⓓ	20.	Ⓐ Ⓑ Ⓒ Ⓓ	26.	Ⓐ Ⓑ Ⓒ Ⓓ
3.	Ⓐ Ⓑ Ⓒ Ⓓ	9.	Ⓐ Ⓑ Ⓒ Ⓓ	15.	Ⓐ Ⓑ Ⓒ Ⓓ	21.	Ⓐ Ⓑ Ⓒ Ⓓ	27.	Ⓐ Ⓑ Ⓒ Ⓓ
4.	Ⓐ Ⓑ Ⓒ Ⓓ	10.	Ⓐ Ⓑ Ⓒ Ⓓ	16.	Ⓐ Ⓑ Ⓒ Ⓓ	22.	Ⓐ Ⓑ Ⓒ Ⓓ	28.	Ⓐ Ⓑ Ⓒ Ⓓ
5.	Ⓐ Ⓑ Ⓒ Ⓓ	11.	Ⓐ Ⓑ Ⓒ Ⓓ	17.	Ⓐ Ⓑ Ⓒ Ⓓ	23.	Ⓐ Ⓑ Ⓒ Ⓓ	29.	Ⓐ Ⓑ Ⓒ Ⓓ
6.	Ⓐ Ⓑ Ⓒ Ⓓ	12.	Ⓐ Ⓑ Ⓒ Ⓓ	18.	Ⓐ Ⓑ Ⓒ Ⓓ	24.	Ⓐ Ⓑ Ⓒ Ⓓ	30.	Ⓐ Ⓑ Ⓒ Ⓓ

LEARNING OBJECTIVES

➤ Combustion
➤ Controlling fire
➤ Flame and its different types
➤ The structure of candle flame
➤ Fuel efficiency

MULTIPLE CHOICE QUESTIONS

1. Calorific value of a fuel is the heat energy produced when _______.
   (A) one gram of fuel is completely burnt
   (B) hundred grams of fuel is completely burnt
   (C) one kilogram of fuel is completely burnt
   (D) any amount of fuel is completely burnt

2. Which of the following is the combination of acid rain?
   (A) $H_2SO_4 + HNO_3$
   (B) $H_2SO_4 + NO_2$
   (C) $HNO_3 + SO_2$
   (D) Both (B) and (C)

3. Good fuels have _______.
   (A) low ignition temperature and high calorific value
   (B) high ignition temperature and low calorific value
   (C) low ignition temperature and low calorific value
   (D) high ignition temperature and high calorific value

4. Log of wood does not burn very easily but it is easy to burn small pieces of wood dipped in kerosene oil. This is because kerosene oil provides proper _______.
   (A) thermal energy
   (B) heat and air
   (C) ignition temperature
   (D) none of these

5. The chemicals present in fire extinguisher are _______.
   (A) $NaHCO_3$, Na_2CO_3
   (B) H_2SO_4, $NaHCo_3$
   (C) HCl, Na_2CO_3
   (D) HCl, $NaHCo_3$, H_2SO_4

6. Which of these is/are liquid fuel(s)?
   (A) LPG
   (B) CNG
   (C) Petrol
   (D) All of these

7. Which poisonous gas is formed as a result of incomplete combustion?
   (A) Coal gas
   (B) CO_2
   (C) CO
   (D) NO_2

8. The hottest zone of a candle flame is _____.
   (A) non-luminous zone
   (B) luminous zone
   (C) dark zone
   (D) blue zone

9. Which of these fuels has the highest calorific value?
   (A) Hydrogen (B) Petrol
   (C) Coal (D) CNG

10. When hydrocarbon (present in fuels) burns completely, the products formed are ______.
    (A) CO_2, H_2O, energy
    (B) CO, H_2O, air
    (B) O_2, CO_2
    (D) CO, CO_2

11. The resulting products in the case of incomplete combustion of methane due to insufficient supply of oxygen are ______.
    (A) CO, H_2O
    (B) CO, H_2O, energy
    (C) CO_2, energy
    (D) H_2O, energy

12. For combustion to take place, we need ______.
    (A) combustible substance
    (B) oxygen in sufficient supply
    (C) ignition temperature
    (D) all of these

13. To extinguish a flame, which of these methods is used?
    (A) cut the air supply
    (B) reduce temperature below ignition temperature
    (C) remove the combustible matter
    (D) all of these

14. The combustion in which a material bursts into flames without the application of heat is called ______.
    (A) rapid combustion
    (B) explosion
    (C) spontaneous combustion
    (D) slow combustion

15. Which of these materials represents spontaneous combustion?
    (A) White chlorine
    (B) White phosphorous

    (C) $KMnO_3$
    (D) H_2SO_4

16. Which of these is a solid pollutant?
    (A) SPM (B) CO
    (C) CO_2 (D) SO_2

17. SPM, also called dangerous pollutants, means ______.
    (A) suspended particle mixture
    (B) suspended particulate matter
    (C) suspension powder material
    (D) suspended powdered matter

18. The coldest zone of flame is ______ zone.
    (A) luminous (B) non-luminous
    (C) blue (D) black

19. In which zone is carbon monoxide burns with a blue colour at the base of the wick?
    (A) luminous zone
    (B) black zone
    (C) blue zone
    (D) non-luminous zone

20. The SI unit of calorific value is ______.
    (A) kg/J (B) J/kg
    (C) kJ/kg (D) J kg s^{-1}

21. The calorific value of petrol is ______.
    (A) 15000 kJ/kg
    (B) 55,000 kJ/kg
    (C) 45,000 kJ/kg
    (D) 1,50,000 kJ/kg

22. A fuel is considered good if it ______.
    (A) has low ignition temperature
    (B) has high calorific value
    (C) is safe to store, easy to handle and pollution free
    (D) all of these

23. Burning of magnesium is an example of which combustion?
    (A) rapid combustion
    (B) explosion
    (C) spontaneous combustion
    (D) slow combustion

24. The most commonly used fire extinguisher is soda-acid fire extinguisher. Cylinder is filled with a solution of ________.
  (A) Sodium chloride
  (B) Sodium bicarbonate
  (C) Sulphuric acid
  (D) Na_2HCO_2

25. Which of these is gaseous fuel?
  (A) Wood gas   (B) LPG
  (C) Coal   (D) Alcohol

HOTS (ACHIEVERS SECTION)

26. The combustion in a match stick is started by this chemical ________.
  (A) Potassium chloride
  (B) Antimony sulphide
  (C) Phosphorous
  (D) Sodium sulphate

27. Which of the following is most harmful for human body?
  (A) CO
  (B) CO_2
  (C) Oxides of nitrogen
  (D) Lead compounds

28. Fly ash is produced by the burning of ______.
  (A) Petroleum
  (B) Natural gas
  (C) Coal
  (D) All of these

29. 'Firework' is an example of
  (A) rapid combustion
  (B) explosion
  (C) spontaneous combustion
  (D) slow combustion

30. The calorific value of 'hydrogen' is
  (A) 50,000 kJ/kg
  (B) 55,000 kJ/kg
  (C) 1,50,000 kJ/kg
  (D) 6,000 kJ/kg

Darken Your Choice with HB Pencil

1.	(A) (B) (C) (D)	7.	(A) (B) (C) (D)	13.	(A) (B) (C) (D)	19	(A) (B) (C) (D)	25.	(A) (B) (C) (D)
2.	(A) (B) (C) (D)	8.	(A) (B) (C) (D)	14.	(A) (B) (C) (D)	20.	(A) (B) (C) (D)	26.	(A) (B) (C) (D)
3.	(A) (B) (C) (D)	9.	(A) (B) (C) (D)	15.	(A) (B) (C) (D)	21.	(A) (B) (C) (D)	27.	(A) (B) (C) (D)
4.	(A) (B) (C) (D)	10.	(A) (B) (C) (D)	16.	(A) (B) (C) (D)	22.	(A) (B) (C) (D)	28.	(A) (B) (C) (D)
5.	(A) (B) (C) (D)	11.	(A) (B) (C) (D)	17.	(A) (B) (C) (D)	23.	(A) (B) (C) (D)	29.	(A) (B) (C) (D)
6.	(A) (B) (C) (D)	12.	(A) (B) (C) (D)	18.	(A) (B) (C) (D)	24.	(A) (B) (C) (D)	30.	(A) (B) (C) (D)

CONSERVATION OF PLANTS AND ANIMALS

MULTIPLE CHOICE QUESTIONS

1. Project tiger was launched in India in
   ________.
   (A) 1989 (B) 1970
   (C) 1973 (D) 1998

2. The plants found in a particular region are called ________.
   (A) Flora (B) Fauna
   (C) Species (D) Local plants

3. If all trees in a forest are cut, it will lead to ________.
   (A) erosion of soil (B) desertification
   (C) both (A) and (B) (D) none of these

4. Cattles should be stopped from ________ in order to conserve forests.
   (A) overgrazing (B) wandering
   (C) eating grass (D) all of these

5. Which one of these is not included in wildlife?
   (A) elephant (B) leopard
   (C) horse (D) lion

6. Which one of the following is not a conservation category of wildlife?
   (A) extinct (B) endangered
   (C) endemic (D) vulnerable

7. Wildlife conservation in natural habitats is done in ________.
   (A) sanctuaries
   (B) national parks
   (C) biosphere reserves
   (D) all of these

8. Wildlife in India is diversity in because of diverse ________.
   (A) species (B) habitat
   (C) culture (D) climate

9. Which of these is not caused by deforestation?
   (A) desertification
   (B) global warming
   (C) storms
   (D) reduction in groundwater

10. If all animals disappeared from an area, they are called ________.
    (A) extinct (B) endangered
    (C) vulnerable (D) endemic

11. Total number of national parks in India are ________.
    (A) 15 (B) 25
    (C) 55 (D) 89

12. Which of these animals is an endangered species?
    (A) Tiger (B) Elephant
    (C) Peacock (D) Monkey

13. Dodo is a/an ———.
   (A) endangered species
   (B) extinct species
   (C) vulnerable species
   (D) critically endangered species
14. WWF stands for ———.
   (A) world wide fund
   (B) wild world forest
   (C) world wild fund
   (D) world wresting foundation
15. WWF works in the field of ———.
   (A) wildlife conservation
   (B) forest conservation
   (C) child labour abolition
   (D) water conservation
16. Different species are classified into different threat categories for different countries in the book named ———.
   (A) yellow data book
   (B) blue data book
   (C) red data book
   (D) green data book
17. Which of these is an endangered animal?
   (A) Dodo   (B) Asiatic lion
   (C) Gorilla   (D) Sikkim stag
18. In India, Asiatic lions are found in ———.
   (A) Gir forest   (B) Sunderbans
   (C) Sahara Desert   (D) Assam
19. The flora and fauna of a country are among the most important ——— natural resources.
   (A) renewable   (B) non-renewable
   (C) perishable   (D) exhaustible
20. Species which are confined to a restricted area on the earth are known as ———.
   (A) epidemic species
   (B) endemic species
   (C) geographical species
   (D) local species
21. A large protected area, set aside for conservation of wildlife, plants and animal species and the traditional life of the tribals living there, is termed as ———.
   (A) Biological reserve
   (B) Botanical reserve
   (C) Geographical reserve
   (D) Biosphere reserve
22. The National Park which is located in Rajasthan is ———.
   (A) Corbett National Park
   (B) Kanha National Park
   (C) Satpura National Park
   (D) Sariska National Park
23. Animals that begin to die, as they cannot adjust themselves to environmental changes, resulting in their population becoming very small, are called ———.
   (A) extinct
   (B) endangered
   (C) critically endangered
   (D) vulnerable
24. Forests can be conserved by way of ———.
   (A) planned harvesting of trees
   (B) afforestation and control of overgrazing
   (C) protection from fire, pests and insect
   (D) all of these
25. Wildlife can be conserved by ———.
   (A) habitat preservation
   (B) building wildlife sanctuaries
   (C) implementing hunting regulations
   (D) all of these
26. The wide range of different animal species, plants, grass, birds in an area constitute ——— of that area.
   (A) biodiversity   (B) biosphere
   (C) flora and fauna   (D) both (A) and (C)
27. Illegal hunting of animals are called ———.
   (A) encroaching   (B) poaching
   (C) phishing   (D) hunting
28. IUCN stands for ———.
   (A) International Unity of Conserving Nature
   (B) Internation Union for Cultivating Nature

(C) International Union for Conservation of Natural Resources

(D) Internation Union for Controlling Natural Hazards

29. Which of the following wild animals is not listed in the Red Data Book in India?

(A) Black bunch

(B) Flying squirrel

(C) Tiger

(D) Leopard

30. Which organization maintains a Red List?

(A) UNO

(B) WWF

(C) IUCN

(D) Red Book Society

HOTS (ACHIEVERS SECTION)

31. Name a biosphere reserve where the plants and animals are similar to those of the upper Himalayan ranges and lower western ghats.

(A) Nanda Devi Biosphere Reserve

(B) Kaziranga Biosphere Reserve

(C) Pachmarhi Biosphere Reserve

(D) Dudhwa National Park

32. Which of the following activities are prohibited in national parks, sanctuaries and biosphere reserves?

(A) Poaching   (B) Hunting

(C) Felling trees   (D) All of these

33. Name the areas where animals are protected from any disturbance to them and their habitat.

(A) Sanctuary   (B) Biodiversity

(C) Palaces   (D) Beach

34. Name the areas reserved for wildlife where they can freely use the habitats and national resources.

(A) National parks

(B) Sanctuary

(C) Oceans

(D) Homes

35. Large areas of protected land for conservation of wildlife, plant and animal resources and traditional life of the tribals living in the area are referred to as

(A) biosphere reserves

(B) sanctuaries

(C) national parks

(D) all of these

—Darken Your Choice with HB Pencil—

1.	Ⓐ Ⓑ Ⓒ Ⓓ	8.	Ⓐ Ⓑ Ⓒ Ⓓ	15.	Ⓐ Ⓑ Ⓒ Ⓓ	22	Ⓐ Ⓑ Ⓒ Ⓓ	29.	Ⓐ Ⓑ Ⓒ Ⓓ
2.	Ⓐ Ⓑ Ⓒ Ⓓ	9.	Ⓐ Ⓑ Ⓒ Ⓓ	16.	Ⓐ Ⓑ Ⓒ Ⓓ	23.	Ⓐ Ⓑ Ⓒ Ⓓ	30.	Ⓐ Ⓑ Ⓒ Ⓓ
3.	Ⓐ Ⓑ Ⓒ Ⓓ	10.	Ⓐ Ⓑ Ⓒ Ⓓ	17.	Ⓐ Ⓑ Ⓒ Ⓓ	24.	Ⓐ Ⓑ Ⓒ Ⓓ	31.	Ⓐ Ⓑ Ⓒ Ⓓ
4.	Ⓐ Ⓑ Ⓒ Ⓓ	11.	Ⓐ Ⓑ Ⓒ Ⓓ	18.	Ⓐ Ⓑ Ⓒ Ⓓ	25.	Ⓐ Ⓑ Ⓒ Ⓓ	32.	Ⓐ Ⓑ Ⓒ Ⓓ
5.	Ⓐ Ⓑ Ⓒ Ⓓ	12.	Ⓐ Ⓑ Ⓒ Ⓓ	19.	Ⓐ Ⓑ Ⓒ Ⓓ	26.	Ⓐ Ⓑ Ⓒ Ⓓ	33.	Ⓐ Ⓑ Ⓒ Ⓓ
6.	Ⓐ Ⓑ Ⓒ Ⓓ	13.	Ⓐ Ⓑ Ⓒ Ⓓ	20.	Ⓐ Ⓑ Ⓒ Ⓓ	27.	Ⓐ Ⓑ Ⓒ Ⓓ	34.	Ⓐ Ⓑ Ⓒ Ⓓ
7.	Ⓐ Ⓑ Ⓒ Ⓓ	14.	Ⓐ Ⓑ Ⓒ Ⓓ	21.	Ⓐ Ⓑ Ⓒ Ⓓ	28.	Ⓐ Ⓑ Ⓒ Ⓓ	35.	Ⓐ Ⓑ Ⓒ Ⓓ

CELL-STRUCTURE AND FUNCTIONS

LEARNING OBJECTIVES

➤ Cellular organization in humans
➤ The role of cell in maintaining life
➤ Different cell organelles and their functions

MULTIPLE CHOICE QUESTIONS

1. The egg of a hen is a __________.
   (A) tissue   (B) cell
   (C) organ   (D) organ system
2. The structural and functional unit of all living beings is __________.
   (A) Cell   (B) Amoeba
   (C) Bacteria   (D) Nucleus
3. Which of these is multicellular?
   (A) Amoeba   (B) Paramecium
   (C) Bacteria   (D) Mushroom
4. Which of these is not present in animal cells?
   (A) Plastid   (B) Large vacuoles
   (C) Cell wall   (D) All of these
5. Which instrument is used to see onion peel cells on a slide?
   (A) Stethoscope   (B) Bioscope
   (C) Microscope   (D) Telescope
6. The cell organelle that contains chlorophyll and is present in plant cells is __________.
   (A) Mitochondria   (B) Chloroplast
   (C) Large Vacuole   (D) Nucleus
7. Which of these is not present in an animal cell?
   (A) Mitochondria   (B) Cell membrane
   (C) Chloroplast   (D) Nucleus
8. A cell contains __________.
   (A) cytoplasm   (B) nucleus
   (C) chromosome   (D) all of these
9. Which of these is called the control centre of a cell?
   (A) nucleus   (B) cytoplasm
   (C) mitochondria   (D) protoplasm
10. A cell can be __________.
    (A) Eukaryotic cell
    (B) Prokaryotic cell
    (C) Both (A) and (B)
    (D) None of these
11. Which organelles are responsible for energy production in a cell?
    (A) mitochondria   (B) vacuoles
    (C) chloroplast   (D) golgi bodies
12. Which of these is a jelly-like substance found in a cell?
    (A) chloroplast   (B) cytoplasm
    (C) cell membrane   (D) plastid
13. The substance used to stain human cells to observe them clearly under a microscope is __________.

(A) water   (B) ink
(C) iodine   (D) all of these

14. The cytoplasm and the nucleus together make up the ________.
    (A) chloroplast   (B) protoplasm
    (C) mitochondria   (D) cell

15. The spiral band in the spirogyra cell is ________.
    (A) nucleus   (B) cytoplasm
    (C) mitochondria   (D) chloroplast

16. Which of these is not asserted in the cell theory?
    (A) Cells are the basic structural units of a living organism.
    (B) All cells are identical in shape and size.
    (C) New cells are formed due to division in odd cells.
    (D) The way an organism functions depends on the way the cells work.

17. The cell with cytoplasm in it is ________.
    (A) parenchyma   (B) sclerid
    (C) sclerenchyma   (D) cork cell

18. In which of these does a single cell not perform all life functions?
    (A) amoeba   (B) mosquito
    (C) euglena   (D) bacteria

19. Similar type of cells specialized for a particular function form a/an ________.
    (A) organ   (B) cell membrane
    (C) tissue   (D) golgi body

20. Which of these unicellular organisms has no definite shape?
    (A) amoeba   (B) euglena
    (C) bacteria   (D) paramecium

21. The cork-piece slide shows ________.
    (A) living cells
    (B) dead cells
    (C) cells with cytoplasm
    (D) no cells

22. The material between cell membrane and nucleus is called ________.

(A) cytoplasm   (B) chloroplast
(C) mitochondria   (D) vacuole

23. Columnar epithelium cells are ________.
    (A) cube like   (B) cylindrical
    (C) column-like   (D) falt

24. Align and branched animal cell is ________.
    (A) Mused cell
    (B) Reeve cell
    (C) Epithelial cell
    (D) Cartilage cell

25. Which is the longest cell in human body?
    (A) Nerve cell   (B) Brain cell
    (C) Skin cell   (D) None of these

26. Which is the largest cell in the world?
    (A) turkey cell   (B) peafowl
    (C) hen   (D) ostrich egg

27. Glandular cells in epithelium have ________.
    (A) epithelial cells
    (B) goblet cells
    (C) turkey cells
    (D) both (A) and (C)

28. Which the following unicellular organism has two nucleuses?
    (A) Paramecium
    (B) Euglena
    (C) Amoeba
    (D) Chlymadomonas

29. Slides can be prepared and studied under ________.
    (A) dissecting microscope
    (B) compound microscope
    (C) both (A) and (B)
    (D) none of these

30. The smallest cell in living word is ________.
    (A) Red blood cell
    (B) Mycoplasma
    (C) Yeast
    (D) None of these

31. Which of the following organelles acts as digestive system within the cell?
    (A) Golgi bodies (B) Centrosomes
    (C) Lysosomes (D) Mitochondria

32. A group of similar cells combine to form
    (A) tissue (B) organ
    (C) organisms (D) organelles

33. The organism containing only a single cell is called
    (A) unicellular organism
    (B) multicellular organism
    (C) organelle
    (D) all of these

34. Cell walls is found in
    (A) plant cells only
    (B) animal cells only
    (C) both (A) and (B)
    (D) none of them

35. The empty blank looking structures in the cytoplasm is
    (A) vacuoles
    (B) plastids
    (C) plasma membrane
    (D) nucleus

Darken Your Choice with HB Pencil

1.	Ⓐ Ⓑ Ⓒ Ⓓ	8.	Ⓐ Ⓑ Ⓒ Ⓓ	15.	Ⓐ Ⓑ Ⓒ Ⓓ	22	Ⓐ Ⓑ Ⓒ Ⓓ	29.	Ⓐ Ⓑ Ⓒ Ⓓ
2.	Ⓐ Ⓑ Ⓒ Ⓓ	9.	Ⓐ Ⓑ Ⓒ Ⓓ	16.	Ⓐ Ⓑ Ⓒ Ⓓ	23.	Ⓐ Ⓑ Ⓒ Ⓓ	30.	Ⓐ Ⓑ Ⓒ Ⓓ
3.	Ⓐ Ⓑ Ⓒ Ⓓ	10.	Ⓐ Ⓑ Ⓒ Ⓓ	17.	Ⓐ Ⓑ Ⓒ Ⓓ	24.	Ⓐ Ⓑ Ⓒ Ⓓ	31.	Ⓐ Ⓑ Ⓒ Ⓓ
4.	Ⓐ Ⓑ Ⓒ Ⓓ	11.	Ⓐ Ⓑ Ⓒ Ⓓ	18.	Ⓐ Ⓑ Ⓒ Ⓓ	25.	Ⓐ Ⓑ Ⓒ Ⓓ	32.	Ⓐ Ⓑ Ⓒ Ⓓ
5.	Ⓐ Ⓑ Ⓒ Ⓓ	12.	Ⓐ Ⓑ Ⓒ Ⓓ	19.	Ⓐ Ⓑ Ⓒ Ⓓ	26.	Ⓐ Ⓑ Ⓒ Ⓓ	33.	Ⓐ Ⓑ Ⓒ Ⓓ
6.	Ⓐ Ⓑ Ⓒ Ⓓ	13.	Ⓐ Ⓑ Ⓒ Ⓓ	20.	Ⓐ Ⓑ Ⓒ Ⓓ	27.	Ⓐ Ⓑ Ⓒ Ⓓ	34.	Ⓐ Ⓑ Ⓒ Ⓓ
7.	Ⓐ Ⓑ Ⓒ Ⓓ	14.	Ⓐ Ⓑ Ⓒ Ⓓ	21.	Ⓐ Ⓑ Ⓒ Ⓓ	28.	Ⓐ Ⓑ Ⓒ Ⓓ	35.	Ⓐ Ⓑ Ⓒ Ⓓ

REPRODUCTION IN ANIMALS

LEARNING OBJECTIVES

➤ Asexual and sexual reproduction
➤ The fertilization process in human
➤ External and internal fertilization

MULTIPLE CHOICE QUESTIONS

1. Which of the following is a hermaphrodite animal?
   (A) Frog   (B) Sheep
   (C) Earthworm   (D) Snake

2. Which of these are male reproductive organs in human beings?
   (A) Testes   (B) Sperms
   (C) Ova   (D) Ovaries

3. Animals reproduce by __________.
   (A) asexual mode
   (B) sexual mode
   (C) both (A) and (B)
   (D) vegetative mode

4. Turkey and ostrich reproduces by ________.
   (A) laying eggs
   (B) giving birth to young ones
   (C) both (A) and (B)
   (D) none of these

5. Sperm and egg fuse together to form ______.
   (A) Infant   (B) Placenta
   (C) Embryo   (D) Zygote

6. Animals that give birth to babies are called __________.
   (A) Oviparous
   (B) Viviparous
   (C) Metamorphoses
   (D) Hermaphrodite

7. In ________ the offspring grows out of the parent's body.
   (A) Hydra   (B) Amoeba
   (C) Paramecium   (D) Human

8. The transformation of larva into an adult through drastic changes is called ________.
   (A) Osmoporesis   (B) Dialysis
   (C) Metamorphosis (D) Transformation

9. Onset of sexual maturity in human beings is called __________.
   (A) Adolescence   (B) Maturity
   (C) Reproduction   (D) Puberty

10. ______ reproduction involves the production of new organisms by just one parent.
    (A) External   (B) Asexual
    (C) Monosexual   (D) Sexual

11. In humans, fertilization occurs in __________.
    (A) oviduct   (B) uterus
    (C) ovary   (D) vagina

12. Hormones are secreted by __________.
(A) exocrine glands (B) cells
(C) endocrine glands (D) tissues

13. The fusion process of sperm and ovum is known as __________.
(A) Metamorphosis (B) Fertilization
(C) Reproduction   (D) Cultivation

14. Which of the following organisms reproduces by binary fission?
(A) Hydra   (B) Yeast
(C) Amoeba   (D) Sea anemone

15. In a mosquito, the eggs hatch to produce __________.
(A) Pupa   (B) Larva
(C) Embryo   (D) Adult mosquito

16. Amoeba reproduces by __________.
(A) budding
(B) fragmentation
(C) binary fusion
(D) sexual reproduction

17. Which of these reproduces by budding process?
(A) Hydra   (B) Spirogyra
(C) Sponge   (D) Mushroom

18. In multicellular organisms, development of the embryo occurs by __________.
(A) cell division
(B) cell differentiation
(C) both (A) and (B)
(D) none of these

19. Humans start becoming sexually mature at the age of __________.
(A) 10 – 16   (B) 3 – 5
(C) 13 – 18   (D) 25 – 30

20. The baby sheep DOLLY was cloned and developed from a cell taken from the _____ gland of a female sheep, and an unfertilized egg taken from another female sheep.
(A) Pituitary   (B) Endocrine
(C) Exocrine   (D) Mammary

21. Which of the following animals does not show metamorphosis?
(A) Fish   (B) Frog
(C) Silk moth   (D) Mosquito

22. The natural process of giving birth to young ones of their own kind is termed as __________.
(A) production   (B) metamorphosis
(C) reproduction   (D) fertilization

23. Which one is the reproductive organ in flowering plants?
(A) Leaf   (B) Flower
(C) Bud   (D) Seed

24. Which of these is a hermaphrodite?
(A) Flower   (B) Bird
(C) Amoeba   (D) Man

25. Flower has the __________ which produces the egg cell and the __________ which produces the male gamete in the same flower.
(A) stamen, sepal   (B) pistil, stamen
(C) stamen, pistil   (D) pistil, whole

26. Which of these reproduce by external fertilization?
(A) Starfish   (B) Jelly fish
(C) Frog   (D) All of these

27. Which of these reproduce by internal fertilization?
(A) Bird   (B) Whale
(C) Human   (D) All of these

28. Which of these is not a viviparous animal?
(A) Goat   (B) Tiger
(C) Snake   (D) Dog

29. How many weeks does it take for an embryo of a hen to develop into a chick?
(A) One week   (B) Two weeks
(C) Three weeks   (D) 12 days

30. Which reproduction system is common in flowering plants and humans?
(A) Sperm ducts   (B) Ovary
(C) Anther   (D) Style

Directions (31–33): Answer the questions given below on the basis of given diagram.

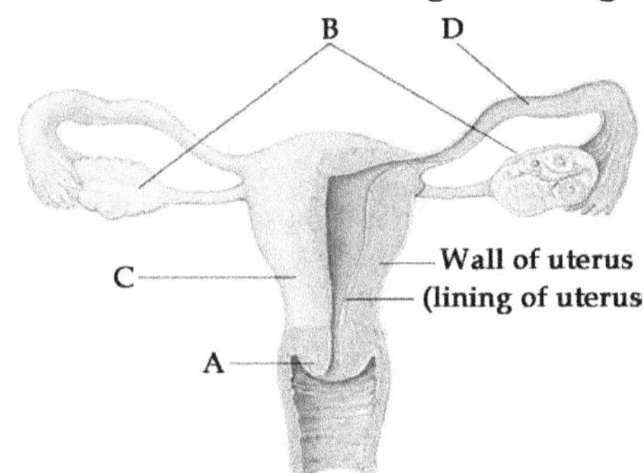

Reproductive System of Human Female

31. Which of the following produces one mature ovum each after four weeks?

(A) A   (B) B
(C) C   (D) D

32. In which of the following sterilized embryo develops into baby foetus?

(A) A   (B) B
(C) C   (D) D

33. Which of the following carries the eggs toward uterus?

(A) A   (B) B
(C) C   (D) D

34. In the list of animals given below, hen is the odd one out.

'human being, cow, dog, hen'

The reason for this is

(A) it undergoes internal fertilisation
(B) it is oviparous
(C) it is viviparous
(D) it undergoes external fertilisation

35. Animals exhibiting external fertilisation produce a large number of gametes. Pick the appropriate reason from the following

(A) The animals are small in size and want to produce more offsprings.
(B) Food is available in plenty in water.
(C) To ensure better chance of fertilisation.
(D) Water promotes production of large number of gametes.

---

1. Ⓐ Ⓑ Ⓒ Ⓓ	8. Ⓐ Ⓑ Ⓒ Ⓓ	15. Ⓐ Ⓑ Ⓒ Ⓓ	22 Ⓐ Ⓑ Ⓒ Ⓓ	29. Ⓐ Ⓑ Ⓒ Ⓓ
2. Ⓐ Ⓑ Ⓒ Ⓓ	9. Ⓐ Ⓑ Ⓒ Ⓓ	16. Ⓐ Ⓑ Ⓒ Ⓓ	23. Ⓐ Ⓑ Ⓒ Ⓓ	30. Ⓐ Ⓑ Ⓒ Ⓓ
3. Ⓐ Ⓑ Ⓒ Ⓓ	10. Ⓐ Ⓑ Ⓒ Ⓓ	17. Ⓐ Ⓑ Ⓒ Ⓓ	24. Ⓐ Ⓑ Ⓒ Ⓓ	31. Ⓐ Ⓑ Ⓒ Ⓓ
4. Ⓐ Ⓑ Ⓒ Ⓓ	11. Ⓐ Ⓑ Ⓒ Ⓓ	18. Ⓐ Ⓑ Ⓒ Ⓓ	25. Ⓐ Ⓑ Ⓒ Ⓓ	32. Ⓐ Ⓑ Ⓒ Ⓓ
5. Ⓐ Ⓑ Ⓒ Ⓓ	12. Ⓐ Ⓑ Ⓒ Ⓓ	19. Ⓐ Ⓑ Ⓒ Ⓓ	26. Ⓐ Ⓑ Ⓒ Ⓓ	33. Ⓐ Ⓑ Ⓒ Ⓓ
6. Ⓐ Ⓑ Ⓒ Ⓓ	13. Ⓐ Ⓑ Ⓒ Ⓓ	20. Ⓐ Ⓑ Ⓒ Ⓓ	27. Ⓐ Ⓑ Ⓒ Ⓓ	34. Ⓐ Ⓑ Ⓒ Ⓓ
7. Ⓐ Ⓑ Ⓒ Ⓓ	14. Ⓐ Ⓑ Ⓒ Ⓓ	21. Ⓐ Ⓑ Ⓒ Ⓓ	28. Ⓐ Ⓑ Ⓒ Ⓓ	35. Ⓐ Ⓑ Ⓒ Ⓓ

FORCE AND PRESSURE 

LEARNING OBJECTIVES

➤ The forces between two objects
➤ Variation of atmospheric pressure
➤ The pressure exerted by fluids and liquids

MULTIPLE CHOICE QUESTIONS

1. Which of these is a contact force?
   (A) Magnetic force
   (B) Frictional force
   (C) Electrostatic force
   (D) Gravitational force

2. The force exerted by the earth on a body is called __________ of the body.
   (A) mass   (B) weight
   (C) pressure   (D) force

3. Atmospheric pressure is the pressure exerted by __________.
   (A) solid   (B) gases in air
   (C) liquid of rivers   (D) atmosphere

4. Which of these cannot be changed by the force acting on an object?
   (A) Mass
   (B) Shape
   (C) State of rest
   (D) Direction motion

5. Which of the following is TRUE for the pressure exerted by a liquid?
   (A) Pressure is independent of depth of the liquid.
   (B) Pressure is always in the downward direction only.
   (C) Pressure is exerted in all directions but downward pressure is greater than sideways pressure.
   (D) At the same depth, pressure is same in all directions.

6. As pressure is the force applied per unit area, so __________.
   (A) school bags have narrow straps
   (B) pointed nails are easier to hammer in wood
   (C) all cutting tools have blunt cutting edge
   (D) tractors have thin and flat tyres

7. If the force is constant, then pressure is __________ proportional to area.
   (A) inversely   (B) directly
   (C) not   (D) none of these

8. If no force acts on a body, it will __________.
   (A) break
   (B) get deformed
   (C) move with increasing speed
   (D) either remain at rest or move with the same speed

9. Let us take a beaker filled with water. We increase the pressure on air in the beaker

at its bottom. The pressure is transmitted in ——————.
(A) west direction
(B) east direction
(C) equally in all directions
(D) south direction

10. A force of 15N acts on an area of 1m². The force is kept the same, but the area is reduced to half. What will happen to the pressure?
(A) Pressure get doubled
(B) Pressure reduced to half
(C) Pressure does not change
(D) Pressure increases by 1.5 times

11. For a force to come into play, the two objects must ——————.
(A) be placed apart
(B) always move together in same direction
(C) interact with each other
(D) all of these

12. Force of friction ——————.
(A) is a contact force
(B) acts in the direction same or opposite to direction of motion
(C) is small if surface are smooth
(D) all of these

13. The study of causes of motion of an object is called ——————.
(A) physics
(B) dynamics
(C) kinetics
(D) mechanics

14. Which of these is not true about force?
(A) It has magnitude.
(B) It has direction.
(C) It is scalar.
(D) It changes the state of motion.

15. What effect does force produce when applied to an object?
(A) It can change the speed or direction of motion of the object.
(B) It can change the state of rest or motion of the object.
(C) It can change the dimension or shape of the object.
(D) All of these

16. Pressure is measured using ——————.
(A) barometer
(B) galvanometer
(C) manometer
(D) none of these

17. Two forces are acting simultaneously on the football and the football still remains static, i.e., at rest. The force is said to be —————— force.
(A) constant
(B) equilibrium
(C) balanced
(D) static

18. The value of atmospheric pressure on the surface of the earth at sea level is ——————.
(A) 1.013×10^5 N/m²
(B) 1.50×10^5 N/m²
(C) 1.013×10^{-5} N/m²
(D) 1.50×10^{-5} N/m²

19. If a set of forces applied on an object move or accelerate the body, then forces are called ——————.
(A) balanced forces
(B) effective forces
(C) unbalanced forces
(D) dynamic forces

20. Muscular force and friction force are ——————.
(A) contact forces
(B) gravitational forces
(C) magnetic forces
(D) distant forces

21. By applying a force of 1N, body of approximately how much mass can we hold in our hand?
(A) 1000g
(B) 100g
(C) 10g
(D) 0.1g

22. Electrostatic forces can be __________.
    (A) attractive
    (B) repulsive
    (C) either (A) or (B)
    (D) neither (A) nor (B)
23. Pressure exerted by a block in standing position is __________ than the pressure exerted by the block in lying position.
    (A) less
    (B) more
    (C) equal
    (D) very less
24. The instrument used to measure the atmospheric pressure is __________.
    (A) Manometer
    (B) Hygrometer
    (C) Lactometer
    (D) Barometer
25. When we press the bulb of a dropper with its nozzle kept in water, air in the dropper is seen to escape in the form of bubbles. Once we release the pressure on the bulb, water rises up in the dropper. The rise of water in the dropper is due to __________.
    (A) pressure of water
    (B) atmospheric pressure
    (C) gravity
    (D) shape of rubber bulb

HOTS (ACHIEVERS SECTION)

26. **Statement 1:** A boy pushes a toy car on the floor. After reaching a distance, the car will be stopped without application of any visible force.

    Statement 2: Frictional force is the force exerted by a surface when an object moves across the surface.
    (A) Statement 1 is true but statement 2 is false.
    (B) Statement 2 is true but statement 1 is false.
    (C) Both statement 1 and statement 2 are true.
    (D) Both statement 1 and statement 2 are true and statement 2 is the correct reason for statement 1.
27. **Statement 1:** The atmospheric pressure changes from place to place and from time to time.

    Statement 2: The temperature and quantity of water vapour in air changes from place to place and time to time.
    (A) Statement 1 is true but statement 2 is false.
    (B) Statement 2 is true but statement 1 is false.
    (C) Both statement 1 and statement 2 are true.
    (D) Both statement 1 and statement 2 are true and statement 2 is the correct reason for statement 1.

Directions (28–30): Fill in the blanks with the appropriate answers.

28. Magnetic, electrostatic and gravitational forces are __________ forces.
    (A) contact   (B) non-contact
    (C) attractive   (D) repulsive
29. __________ is a direct reading instrument which is used for measuring atmospheric pressure.
    (A) Multimeter
    (B) Richter scale
    (C) Aneroid barometer
    (D) None of these

30. A force of 20N is distributed uniformly on one surface of a cube of edge 4 cm. The pressure on this surface is __________.

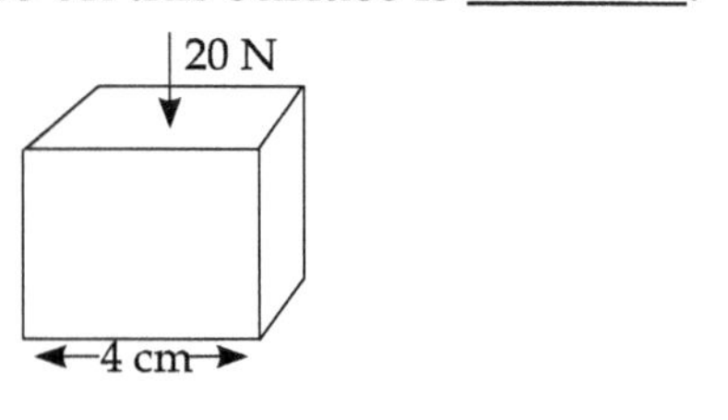

(A) 12,500 Pa

(B) 5000 Pa

(C) 2400 Pa

(D) 1250 Pa

FRICTION

LEARNING OBJECTIVES

- ➤ The phenomenon of friction force and its causes
- ➤ The factors on which the force of friction depends
- ➤ Advantages and disadvantages of friction

MULTIPLE CHOICE QUESTIONS

1. Which of the following represents frictional force?
   (A) $f_r = \mu N$
   (B) $f_r = 6 \pi nr$
   (C) $f_r = \mu Nr$
   (D) $f_r = \mu$

2. Which of these is true about friction?
   (A) It can stop a moving object.
   (B) It can change the direction of a moving object.
   (C) It can make a moving object faster.
   (D) It can change the shape of an object.

3. Two bodies in contact but not moving with respect to each other can exert __________.
   (A) stable friction
   (B) static friction
   (C) limiting friction
   (D) sliding friction

4. Oiling or greasing of moving parts in a machine __________.
   (A) reduces the friction
   (B) changes the friction
   (C) increases the friction
   (D) stops the friction

5. Disadvantage of friction is that __________.
   (A) we can write on paper
   (B) we are able to walk
   (C) we can stop a moving vehicle
   (D) the parts of machine wear and tear

6. A ball moving on a horizontal surface stops because of the __________.
   (A) force of gravity
   (B) force of friction
   (C) atmospheric pressure
   (D) blockage

7. When one object moves over the surface of other object __________.
   (A) surface of only lower object exerts frictional force on the upper object
   (B) surface of both the objects exert force in the direction opposite to each other
   (C) either (A) or (B) can be possible
   (D) none of these

8. Ball bearings are useful because rolling friction is __________.
   (A) less than sliding friction
   (B) more than sliding friction
   (C) equal to sliding friction
   (D) easier to manage friction

9. The smoother the surface is, ______ will be the friction.
   (A) greater
   (B) lesser
   (C) slippery
   (D) smooth

10. Fluid friction can be reduced by __________.
    (A) streamlining   (B) ball bearing
    (C) lubrication   (D) oiling
11. Friction can oppose __________.
    (A) movement   (B) slip
    (C) speed   (D) force of gravity
12. Which of the following is correct regarding friction?
    (A) wastes energy
    (B) wears out the rubbing surface
    (C) generates heat
    (D) all of these
13. Friction is minimized by __________.
    (A) polishing and lubrication
    (B) streamlining
    (C) use of wheels and ball bearings
    (D) all of these
14. Frictional force that fluids exert on an object is called __________.
    (A) brag   (B) blag
    (C) drag   (D) krag
15. The bodies of aeroplanes, missiles, rockets, cars are streamlined to reduce friction with air. This friction force is called __________.
    (A) air resistance
    (B) air friction
    (C) drag
    (D) gravitational resistance
16. The force of friction between two bodies in contact is __________.
    (A) parallel to body position
    (B) parallel to contact surface
    (C) perpendicular to contact surface
    (D) inclined at 45° to contact surface
17. Friction due to water and air can be reduced by suitably designing the shape of the objects. This is called __________.
    (A) ball setting
    (B) frictional adjustment
    (C) streamlining
    (D) figure correction
18. Method of increasing friction is by __________.
    (A) using lubricant
    (B) providing grooves on sole of shoes
    (C) polishing the surfaces
    (D) using ball bearing
19. Sprinkling of powder on the carromboard __________ friction.
    (A) decreases   (B) increases
    (C) does not affect   (D) none of these
20. The force of friction that exists between the surfaces in contact when one body slides over the surface of other body is called __________ friction.
    (A) rolling   (B) static
    (C) sliding   (D) moving
21. Which of these frictions is the least in magnitude?
    (A) static friction   (B) sliding friction
    (C) rolling friction (D) all are equal
22. Which of these frictions is largest in magnitude in comparison to other frictions?
    (A) rolling   (B) sliding
    (C) static   (D) all are equal
23. Which of these statements is not correct?
    (A) A ball moving on a horizontal surface stops due to force of friction.
    (B) Force of friction helps us to walk on ground.
    (C) Wheels are spherical in shape as rolling friction is less than sliding friction.
    (D) Tyres have grooves to reduce the friction.
24. What type of friction does not allow two surfaces to slide upon one another?
    (A) fluid friction   (B) static friction
    (C) sliding friction (D) drag
25. When two bodies are in contact, friction opposes the relative motion between __________.
    (A) the upper surfaces
    (B) the lower surfaces
    (C) both the surfaces in contact
    (D) none of these

26. See the figure given below and find the position where static friction is maximum.

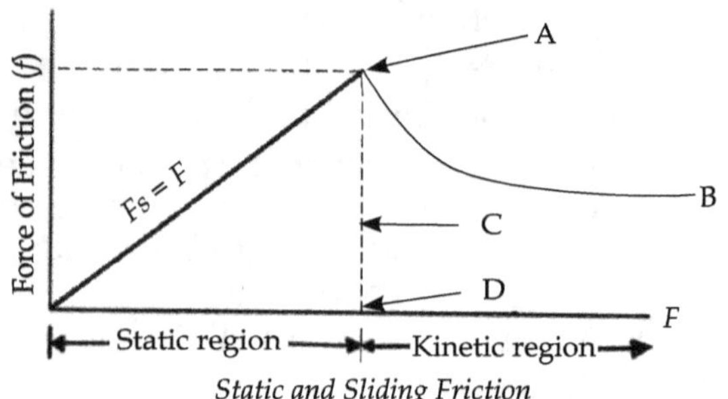

Static and Sliding Friction

(A) A   (B) B
(C) C   (D) D

27. Luis throws four stones having the same weight on four different surfaces. The surfaces are icy, dry, sandy, and cemented. He throws each stone with the same force. On which of the given surfaces will the stone go the maximum distance before it stops?

(A) Icy surface
(B) Dry surface
(C) Sandy surface
(D) Cemented surface

28. The joints of Latif's garage door are producing sound. To solve this problem, he must apply

(A) Saw dust in the joints of the door
(B) Water in the joints of the door
(C) Sand in the joints of the door
(D) Oil in the joints of the door

29. In a cycling race, it is observed that a cyclist normally bends his body forward (as shown in the given figure).

The cyclist bends in order to
(A) Feel comfortable
(B) Reduce his weight
(C) Reduce the air drag
(D) Increase energy consumption

30. Which of the following actions does not increase friction?

(A) Threading tires
(B) Grinding on stones
(C) Making spikes on shoes
(D) Powdering a carrom board

Darken Your Choice with HB Pencil

1.	Ⓐ Ⓑ Ⓒ Ⓓ	7.	Ⓐ Ⓑ Ⓒ Ⓓ	13.	Ⓐ Ⓑ Ⓒ Ⓓ	19	Ⓐ Ⓑ Ⓒ Ⓓ	25.	Ⓐ Ⓑ Ⓒ Ⓓ
2.	Ⓐ Ⓑ Ⓒ Ⓓ	8.	Ⓐ Ⓑ Ⓒ Ⓓ	14.	Ⓐ Ⓑ Ⓒ Ⓓ	20.	Ⓐ Ⓑ Ⓒ Ⓓ	26.	Ⓐ Ⓑ Ⓒ Ⓓ
3.	Ⓐ Ⓑ Ⓒ Ⓓ	9.	Ⓐ Ⓑ Ⓒ Ⓓ	15.	Ⓐ Ⓑ Ⓒ Ⓓ	21.	Ⓐ Ⓑ Ⓒ Ⓓ	27.	Ⓐ Ⓑ Ⓒ Ⓓ
4.	Ⓐ Ⓑ Ⓒ Ⓓ	10.	Ⓐ Ⓑ Ⓒ Ⓓ	16.	Ⓐ Ⓑ Ⓒ Ⓓ	22.	Ⓐ Ⓑ Ⓒ Ⓓ	28.	Ⓐ Ⓑ Ⓒ Ⓓ
5.	Ⓐ Ⓑ Ⓒ Ⓓ	11.	Ⓐ Ⓑ Ⓒ Ⓓ	17.	Ⓐ Ⓑ Ⓒ Ⓓ	23.	Ⓐ Ⓑ Ⓒ Ⓓ	29.	Ⓐ Ⓑ Ⓒ Ⓓ
6.	Ⓐ Ⓑ Ⓒ Ⓓ	12.	Ⓐ Ⓑ Ⓒ Ⓓ	18.	Ⓐ Ⓑ Ⓒ Ⓓ	24.	Ⓐ Ⓑ Ⓒ Ⓓ	30.	Ⓐ Ⓑ Ⓒ Ⓓ

SOUND

LEARNING OBJECTIVES

➤ How sound propagates
➤ The medium for propagation of sound
➤ The construction and working of human ear

MULTIPLE CHOICE QUESTIONS

1. The speed of sound in air is __________.
   (A) 331 m/s   (B) 665 m/s
   (C) 1550 m/s   (D) 173 m/s

2. Sound is produced by a __________.
   (A) moving object
   (B) stationary object
   (C) vibrating object
   (D) rotating object

3. Shrillness of the sound is determined by the _______ of vibration.
   (A) amplitude   (B) frequency
   (C) noise   (D) oscillation

4. The length of vocal cords of a man is about __________.
   (A) 5 mm   (B) 10 mm
   (C) 15 mm   (D) 20 mm

5. Human being can hear two sounds separately and distinctly if they are separated by a time interval of _______ second(s).
   (A) 0.1   (B) 0.01
   (C) 1   (D) 10

6. The quality of two sounds with the same fundamental frequency differs because of the number and relative loudness of the __________.
   (A) sound   (B) harmonics
   (C) pitch   (D) none of these

7. An object vibrates with a frequency of 15 Hz. Which of the following is true?
   (A) It produces sound which we can hear if we strain our ears.
   (B) It produces sound which we can hear.
   (C) It produces sound which we cannot hear.
   (D) It does not produce a sound.

8. Maximum displacement of an oscillating body is called __________.
   (A) time period
   (B) pitch
   (C) amplitude
   (D) harmonics

9. Sound travels faster in solids than in gases because __________.
   (A) sound is a form of energy.
   (B) sound bounces back when reflected to a solid.
   (C) sound cannot travel in gases smoothly.
   (D) molecules of solids are closely packed as compared to gases.

10. The audible range of sound frequencies for human beings is __________.
   (A) 0 Hz – 20 Hz
   (B) 20 Hz – 2000 Hz
   (C) 50 Hz – 5000 Hz
   (D) 20 Hz – 20,000 Hz

11. The to-and-fro motion of a body about its mean position is called __________.
   (A) oscillation   (B) vibration
   (C) fluctuation   (D) rotation

12. Shrillness of the sound, also called as pitch, is determined by which characteristic of sound?
   (A) amplitude   (B) frequency
   (C) harmonics   (D) time period

13. Which surface absorbs sound better?
   (A) hard   (B) smooth
   (C) slippery   (D) soft

14. Prolonged exposure to noise louder than _____ can lead to permanent hearing damage.
   (A) 70 dB   (B) 17 dB
   (C) 7 dB   (D) 700 dB

15. Sounds whose frequencies are greater than 20,000 Hz are called __________.
   (A) infrasonic sounds
   (B) supersonic sound
   (C) ultrasonic sound
   (D) none of these

16. In which of the following materials is the speed of sound maximum?
   (A) air   (B) salty water
   (C) iron   (D) snow

17. Pitch of sound depends on __________.
   (A) amplitude of oscillation
   (B) frequency of oscillation
   (C) both (A) and (B)
   (D) none of these

18. Time taken by an object to complete one oscillation is called __________.
   (A) frequency   (B) time frame
   (C) time period   (D) sonic

19. Which of the following frequencies a man can hear?
   (A) 7 Hz   (B) 18 Hz
   (C) 220 Hz   (D) 50,000 Hz

20. In our ears, the vibrations in the air are picked up by which ear?
   (A) outer ear
   (B) inner ear
   (C) middle ear
   (D) none of these

21. Sound of frequency 320 Hz is of lower pitch than the sound of frequency __________.
   (A) 20 Hz   (B) 256 Hz
   (C) 190 Hz   (D) 370 Hz

22. The quality of sound produced by a tuning fork is different from that produced by a musical instrument because of the difference in __________.
   (A) frequency
   (B) harmonics
   (C) amplitude
   (D) none of these

23. Voice of which of these is likely to have a minimum frequency?
   (A) man   (B) baby boy
   (C) little girl   (D) woman

24. In stringed instruments, frequency of sound produced depends on __________.
   (A) tightness of string
   (B) length of string
   (C) thickness of string
   (D) all of these

25. The astronauts on the moon can see each other but cannot hear each other because __________.
   (A) there is no atmosphere
   (B) the moon is very far from the earth
   (C) there is very low temperature
   (D) the gravitational force does not exist there

26. The speed of sound in steel is __________ the speed of sound in air.
    (A) faster than   (B) slower than
    (C) equals to   (D) can't say

27. The sound is produced due to the __________ in the medium.
    (A) reflection   (B) refraction
    (C) disturbance   (D) None of these

28. __________ is the voice box at the upper end of the wind pipe.
    (A) Larynx   (B) Anvil
    (C) Vocal cords   (D) Cochlea

29. When we say sound travels in a medium, we mean __________.
    (A) the disturbance travels in the medium.
    (B) the medium itself travels.
    (C) the source travels in the medium.
    (D) the particles of the medium travels.

30. The voice of a man, a woman and a child are different due to differences in __________.
    (A) lungs   (B) larynx
    (C) vocal cords   (D) wind pipe

Darken Your Choice with HB Pencil

1.	Ⓐ Ⓑ Ⓒ Ⓓ	7.	Ⓐ Ⓑ Ⓒ Ⓓ	13.	Ⓐ Ⓑ Ⓒ Ⓓ	19	Ⓐ Ⓑ Ⓒ Ⓓ	25.	Ⓐ Ⓑ Ⓒ Ⓓ
2.	Ⓐ Ⓑ Ⓒ Ⓓ	8.	Ⓐ Ⓑ Ⓒ Ⓓ	14.	Ⓐ Ⓑ Ⓒ Ⓓ	20.	Ⓐ Ⓑ Ⓒ Ⓓ	26.	Ⓐ Ⓑ Ⓒ Ⓓ
3.	Ⓐ Ⓑ Ⓒ Ⓓ	9.	Ⓐ Ⓑ Ⓒ Ⓓ	15.	Ⓐ Ⓑ Ⓒ Ⓓ	21.	Ⓐ Ⓑ Ⓒ Ⓓ	27.	Ⓐ Ⓑ Ⓒ Ⓓ
4.	Ⓐ Ⓑ Ⓒ Ⓓ	10.	Ⓐ Ⓑ Ⓒ Ⓓ	16.	Ⓐ Ⓑ Ⓒ Ⓓ	22.	Ⓐ Ⓑ Ⓒ Ⓓ	28.	Ⓐ Ⓑ Ⓒ Ⓓ
5.	Ⓐ Ⓑ Ⓒ Ⓓ	11.	Ⓐ Ⓑ Ⓒ Ⓓ	17.	Ⓐ Ⓑ Ⓒ Ⓓ	23.	Ⓐ Ⓑ Ⓒ Ⓓ	29.	Ⓐ Ⓑ Ⓒ Ⓓ
6.	Ⓐ Ⓑ Ⓒ Ⓓ	12.	Ⓐ Ⓑ Ⓒ Ⓓ	18.	Ⓐ Ⓑ Ⓒ Ⓓ	24.	Ⓐ Ⓑ Ⓒ Ⓓ	30.	Ⓐ Ⓑ Ⓒ Ⓓ

CHEMICAL EFFECTS OF ELECTRIC CURRENT

13

MULTIPLE CHOICE QUESTIONS

1. A body can be charged by _________.
   (A) touching it to a charged body
   (B) rubbing it against another body
   (C) bringing a charged body near it
   (D) all of the above methods

2. Adding solute salt to water _________.
   (A) increases its electrical conductivity
   (B) does not change its conductivity
   (C) decreases its electrical conductivity
   (D) none of these

3. Which of these is not true?
   (A) vinegar is a good conductor of electricity
   (B) carbon rod acts as an electrode
   (C) LED is a conductor
   (D) distilled water is an insulator

4. The gold-leaf electroscope is used to _______.
   (A) detect charge only
   (B) detect, measure and find the nature of charge
   (C) detect and measure charge only
   (D) none of these

5. During electroplating, the metal on which electroplating is to be done should be _________.
   (A) anode
   (B) cathode
   (C) electrolyte
   (D) solution

6. Chromium plating is done on objects like _________.
   (A) handles of almirah
   (B) bicycle parts
   (C) kitchen gas burner
   (D) all of these

7. The process of deposition of a layer of any desired metal on another metallic object by means of electricity is called _________.
   (A) electrolysis
   (B) electrodialysis
   (C) electroplating
   (D) none of these

8. Which of these metals will you electroplate on iron to protect it from rusting and to make it shine?
   (A) copper
   (B) silver
   (C) gold
   (D) chromium

9. The decomposition of an electrolyte on passing electric current is called _________.
   (A) cathode
   (B) dialysis
   (C) electrolysis
   (D) electroplating

10. In which of these is current not conducted by electrons?
   (A) copper   (B) aluminium
   (C) distilled water   (D) mercury
11. When electricity is passed through tap water, the gas which evolved are _________.
   (A) H and O   (B) H and Cl
   (C) O_2 and SO_2 (D) H, Cl and O
12. An electric current brings about chemical changes in most conducting _________.
   (A) solids   (B) liquids
   (C) gases   (D) salts
13. A positively charged body has a _________ of electrons.
   (A) deficit   (B) excess
   (C) absence   (D) any of these
14. To make an electric current flow, two components are necessary. First is the circuit and the second is _________.
   (A) electrodes
   (B) electrons
   (C) electromotive force (emf)
   (D) metal
15. Which of these is a conductor of electricity?
   (A) air   (B) wood
   (C) rubber   (D) none of these
16. Which of these is a conductor of electricity?
   (A) iron   (B) brass
   (C) graphite   (D) all of these
17. Electroplating is based on the phenomenon of _________.
   (A) magnetic effect
   (B) chemical effect of electric current
   (C) flow of electrons
   (D) heating effect
18. A tester is used to test the _________.
   (A) electrical conductivity of liquids
   (B) magnetic effect of emf
   (C) battery/cell power
   (D) electroplating
19. In LED, the shorter lead is attached to _________ terminal and longer lead is attached to the _________ terminal.
   (A) positive, negative
   (B) negative, positive
   (C) any of the (A) or (B)
   (D) none of these
20. The copper gets deposited on the plate connected to the _________ terminal of the battery.
   (A) negative   (B) positive
   (C) neutral   (D) none of these
21. The liquid which does not conduct electricity is _________.
   (A) salt solution   (B) tap water
   (C) distilled water   (D) HCl solution
22. Who invented voltaic cell?
   (A) Alexandra Batter
   (B) Alexinho Volta
   (C) Alexandra Volta
   (D) Aleixinho Batter
23. The flow of electric current, as opposed to conventional current, to be from _________ charged body to the _________ charged body.
   (A) negatively, negatively
   (B) negatively, positively
   (C) positively, positively
   (D) positively, negatively
24. Air, distilled water, plastic, wood, paper, cloth and rubber are the examples of _________.
   (A) insulators   (B) conductors
   (C) semiconductors   (D) material
25. Chromium is extensively used in electroplating because _________.
   (A) it does not corrode
   (B) it is scratch resistant
   (C) both (A) and (B)
   (D) it is the cheapest medium of electroplating

26. Which of the following is not an application of electroplating?
    i. To give a shiny appearance to bath taps, bicycle handle bars, wheel rims etc.
    ii. To prevent the food, kept in an iron can, to come into direct contact with iron.
    (A) Only i   (B) Only ii
    (C) Both i and ii   (D) Neither i or ii

27. A bulb in an electric circuit glows due to __________.
    (A) Chemical effect of current
    (B) Conduction of current
    (C) Magnetic effect of current
    (D) Heating effect of current

28. In a cell, electrons move from __________.
    (A) positive electrode to negative electrode
    (B) negative electrode to positive electrode
    (C) electrons do not move, only negative charge moves from one place to another
    (D) both (A) and (B)

29. The chemical decomposition produced by passing an electric current through a conducting liquid is called:
    (A) Combination   (B) Electroplating
    (C) Electrolysis   (D) All of these
    (e) None of these

30. The metal object on which electroplating is to be done is:
    (A) Connected to the negative terminal of battery
    (B) Connected to the positive terminal of battery
    (C) Not connected to the battery
    (D) Both (A) and (B)

Darken Your Choice with HB Pencil

1.	A B C D	7.	A B C D	13.	A B C D	19	A B C D	25.	A B C D
2.	A B C D	8.	A B C D	14.	A B C D	20.	A B C D	26.	A B C D
3.	A B C D	9.	A B C D	15.	A B C D	21.	A B C D	27.	A B C D
4.	A B C D	10.	A B C D	16.	A B C D	22.	A B C D	28.	A B C D
5.	A B C D	11.	A B C D	17.	A B C D	23.	A B C D	29.	A B C D
6.	A B C D	12.	A B C D	18.	A B C D	24.	A B C D	30.	A B C D

SOME NATURAL PHENOMENA  14

MULTIPLE CHOICE QUESTIONS

1. When two bodies are rubbed against each other _________.
   - (A) they acquire equal and similar charges
   - (B) they acquire equal and opposite charges
   - (C) they acquire unequal and opposite charges
   - (D) they acquire unequal and similar charges

2. Like charges _________.
   - (A) always attract each other
   - (B) sometimes attract each other
   - (C) always repel each other
   - (D) sometimes attract and sometimes repel each other

3. Intensity of an earthquake is measured on _______ scale.
   - (A) Richter
   - (B) Newton
   - (C) Seismic
   - (D) Vector

4. The brilliant flash of light produced in the sky is followed by _________.
   - (A) rain
   - (B) snow
   - (C) hail
   - (D) thunder

5. The solid hard crust of the earth is called _________.
   - (A) Biosphere
   - (B) Lithosphere
   - (C) Magma
   - (D) Lava

6. A body can be charged by _________.
   - (A) friction
   - (B) induction
   - (C) conduction
   - (D) all of these

7. A body can be charged by _________.
   - (A) rubbing it against another body
   - (B) touching it to a charged body
   - (C) bringing a charged body near it
   - (D) all of these

8. The earth's lithosphere is made of how many tectonic plates?
   - (A) 10
   - (B) 15
   - (C) 20
   - (D) 25

9. Lightning conductor is used _________.
   - (A) to protect tall buildings from lightning flashes
   - (B) to measure the strength of lightning
   - (C) to protect the building from earthquake
   - (D) to measure the strength of the earthquake

10. An earthquake of intensity __________ can destroy whole of cities.
    - (A) 4.5 – 6.5
    - (B) 6.5 – 7.0
    - (C) 7.0 – 7.9
    - (D) 8 or above

11. Which of these is not true?
    - (A) Seismic waves are created during earthquake.
    - (B) The characteristics of earthquake waves are recorded on seismogram.
    - (C) The intensity of an earthquake depends on the amount of energy released and the size of seismic waves.
    - (D) none of these.

12. Impacts of an earthquake are __________.
    - (A) fires and tsunami
    - (B) landslides and avalanches
    - (C) shaking and ground rupture
    - (D) all of these

13. The point at which the earthquake originates is known as __________.
    - (A) Tectonic point
    - (B) Seismic focus
    - (C) magma wave
    - (D) mantle

14. Sudden shaking of the earth is called __________.
    - (A) lightning
    - (B) thunder
    - (C) hurricane
    - (D) earthquake

15. The process of discharging atmospheric electricity into the earth by a lightning conductor is called __________.
    - (A) short circuiting
    - (B) electrical neutralization
    - (C) earthing
    - (D) both (B) & (C)

16. The flow of heavy charge through air, accompanied by heat and light is called __________.
    - (A) electric discharge
    - (B) current flow
    - (C) electric wave
    - (D) short circuiting

17. When charged by conduction, a body acquires the ________ charge as the charging body.
    - (A) equal
    - (B) opposite
    - (C) same
    - (D) none of these

18. A lightning conductor is a ________.
    - (A) piece of wire with spikes through which current can flow
    - (B) substance that can be charged by clouds
    - (C) metal rod with spikes, fixed to a building
    - (D) copper plate buried in the ground, below a building

19. To test if a body is charged or not, you will use ________.
    - (A) a positively charged body
    - (B) a negatively charged body
    - (C) another uncharged body
    - (D) a positively and a negatively charged body

20. The instrument used for detecting and measuring charge is called ________.
    - (A) ammeter
    - (B) electroscope
    - (C) electrometer
    - (D) seismometer

21. When a silk cloth is rubbed against a glass rod, silk rod will get ________.
    - (A) a negative charge
    - (B) a positive charge
    - (C) unaffected by rubbing
    - (D) none of these

22. Tsunami is caused due to __________.
   (A) movement in seismic waves
   (B) displacement of tectonic plates
   (C) earthquake in sea
   (D) any of these

23. During a lightning stroke in the forest, one should take shelter __________.
   (A) under a big tree
   (B) in an open park
   (C) under shorter trees
   (D) in open vehicle

24. The point directly above the origin point of an earthquake under the surface of earth is called __________.
   (A) epicenter   (B) seismic front
   (C) seismic focus   (D) magma

25. Seismic waves are of two types – surface waves and __________ waves.
   (A) earth   (B) body
   (C) ground   (D) bottom

26. Which of these is true about lightning?
   (A) A brilliant flash of light is called a spark.
   (B) A single flash of lightning is called lightning bolt.
   (C) Lightning can lead upto a thunderstorm.
   (D) all of these

27. Each increase of 1 on a Richter scale means a ___ fold increase in energy of an earthquake.
   (A) 10   (B) 30
   (C) 20   (D) 50

28. There are two types of surface waves, one is Rayleigh waves. Which one of these is another type of surface wave?
   (A) Force waves
   (B) Love waves
   (C) War waves
   (D) Richter waves

29. The devastating 2001 earthquake in India had its epicenter at __________.
   (A) Kutch
   (B) Jamnagar
   (C) Bhuj
   (D) Rajkot

30. The branch of physics which deals with the study of charges at rest is called __________.
   (A) static electricity
   (B) stable electricity
   (C) static electrolysis
   (D) none of these

HOTS (ACHIEVERS SECTION)

31. The streaks of bright light seen during lightning is essentially the path followed by __________.
   (A) UV rays from the sun
   (B) Accumulated electric charge
   (C) Cosmic rays
   (D) None of these

32. Which of the following is the safest way to protect yourself from lightning?
   (A) Open an umbrella for cover
   (B) Take shelter under a green tree
   (C) Squat low on ground
   (D) Run to a covered shed

33. Acid rain is caused by __________.
   (A) Deforestation
   (B) CO_2
   (C) CO
   (D) Oxides of sulphur and nitrogen

34. When you touch a charged body, the charge flows through you into the earth. What is this called?

   (A) Induction   (B) Conduction
   (C) Capacitance   (D) Earthing

35. When we remove polyester or woolen clothes in dark, we can see a spark and hear a crackling sound. Which of the following is responsible for it?

   (A) Static electricity
   (B) Current electricity
   (C) Positive charge
   (D) Negative charge

1. A B C D	8. A B C D	15. A B C D	22 A B C D	29. A B C D
2. A B C D	9. A B C D	16. A B C D	23. A B C D	30. A B C D
3. A B C D	10. A B C D	17. A B C D	24. A B C D	31. A B C D
4. A B C D	11. A B C D	18. A B C D	25. A B C D	32. A B C D
5. A B C D	12. A B C D	19. A B C D	26. A B C D	33. A B C D
6. A B C D	13. A B C D	20. A B C D	27. A B C D	34. A B C D
7. A B C D	14. A B C D	21. A B C D	28. A B C D	35. A B C D

LIGHT 

LEARNING OBJECTIVES

➤ The reflection of light by plain mirror and spherical mirrors
➤ The phenomenon of bending of light rays and their application
➤ The laws of reflection and images formed by mirrors

MULTIPLE CHOICE QUESTIONS

1. If you stand in front of a plane mirror and scratch your right cheek, your image _______.
   (A) scratches its right cheek
   (B) scratches its left cheek
   (C) scratches both cheeks
   (D) does not scratch at all

2. Image formed by plane mirror is always _______.
   (A) inverted and real
   (B) real and erect
   (C) virtual and of same size
   (D) virtual and enlarged

3. Man observes that the distance between the mirror and his image is 4 m. If he moves 1 m towards the mirror, the distance between him and his image will be _______.
   (A) 6 m   (B) 7 m
   (C) 8 m   (D) 9 m

4. Diffused reflection occurs if a ray of light is reflected by a _______.
   (A) concave mirror
   (B) convex mirror
   (C) plane mirror
   (D) rough surface

5. The image which can only be seen by the eye but cannot be taken on screen is called _______.
   (A) inverted image
   (B) lateral image
   (C) virtual image
   (D) illusionary image

6. Visually challenged persons can read and write using _______.
   (A) periscope
   (B) Braille system
   (C) kaleidoscope
   (D) special spectacles

7. Two plane mirrors are kept at the following angles one by one. In which case is the number of images formed the maximum?
   (A) 30°   (B) 45°
   (C) 60°   (D) 75°

8. Two plane mirrors kept at 60° from each other will form how many images of an object kept between them?
   (A) 3   (B) 5
   (C) 7   (D) 11

9. If medium A is optically denser than medium B, then the speed of light is _______.

(A) the same in both mediums.

(B) higher in medium A than in medium B.

(C) higher in medium B than in medium A.

(D) higher in medium A or B depending on thickness of the two mediums.

10. The splitting of white light into its constituent colours is called _________.

(A) refraction

(B) dispersion

(C) deviation

(D) displacement

11. If a person is suffering from hypermetropia, which object he/she most likely to see blurred?

(A) object 25 cm away

(B) object 10 m away

(C) object 100 m away

(D) object at infinity

12. At what position of the object does a convex lens act as a magnifying glass?

(A) between F and 2F

(B) Beyond F

(C) Between F and O

(D) Beyond 2F

13. A normal eye cannot clearly see objects closer than _________ cm.

(A) 10   (B) 15

(C) 20   (D) 25

14. How many dots does the Braille system use?

(A) 9   (B) 7

(C) 6   (D) 5

15. Which one of these controls the amount of light entering the eye?

(A) pupil

(B) iris

(C) cornea

(D) ciliary muscles

16. When white light passes through a glass prism, it is _________.

(A) deviated and dispersed

(B) deviated but not dispursed

(C) laterally displaced and not dispersed

(D) reflected only

17. Myopia is corrected by using spectacles with _________.

(A) glass slabs

(B) concavo-convex lenses

(C) convex-lenses

(D) concave lenses

18. Because of which reflection do we see objects from every direction?

(A) irregular reflection

(B) diffused reflection

(C) both (A) and (B)

(D) neither (A) nor (B)

19. The second law of reflection states that _________.

(A) $\angle i = \angle r$

(B) incident, normal and reflected ray, all lie in the same plane

(C) the point at which the incident ray strikes the surface is called the point of incidence

(D) $\angle i + \angle r = 180°$

20. The number of images formed by mirror at angle θ to each other is given by _________.

(A) $n = \dfrac{360°}{\theta} + 1$

(B) $n = \left(\dfrac{360°}{\theta} - 90°\right) \times 2$

(C) $n = \dfrac{360°}{\theta} - 1$

(D) $n = 360° \times \theta - 1$

21. In which of these objects is plane mirror used?

(A) as looking glass   (B) In solar cookers

(C) in kaleidoscope   (D) all of these

22. The body which absorbs some light incident on it and reflects the remaining light is __________.

(A) opaque

(B) transparent

(C) shining

(D) rough

23. A light year is the distance that light travels in one year and is equal to __________.

(A) 3.25×10^{12} km

(B) 6.5×10^{12} km

(C) 9.5×10^{12} km

(D) 1.65×10^{12} km

24. Time taken for light to reach from the earth to the sun is __________.

(A) 4.12 minutes

(B) 8.3 minutes

(C) 9.5 minutes

(D) 24 hours

25. The brain of a human being interprets the image as __________.

(A) erect and of correct size

(B) inverted and of correct size

(C) erect but of smaller size

(D) none of these

HOTS (ACHIEVERS SECTION)

26. **Statement 1**: The phenomenon of the persistence of vision is employed in the cinematography.

Statement 2: The image formed on the retina of an eye persists for 1/16th of a second.

(A) Statement 1 is true but statement 2 is false.

(B) Statement 2 is true but statement 1 is false.

(C) Both statement 1 and statement 2 are true.

(D) Both statement 1 and statement 2 are true and statement 2 is the correct reason for statement 1.

27. Which of the following suggestions should not be followed for the caring of eyes?

i. We should always read in dim light.

ii. Always read at the normal distance.

iii. Look at the sun for sometime, everyday in the morning.

iv. We should work in dazzling light.

(A) i and ii   (B) ii and iii

(C) iii and iv   (D) i and iv

28. The persistence of the eye is only for __________.

(A) $\dfrac{1}{16}$ th of a second

(B) $\dfrac{1}{10}$ th of a second

(C) $\dfrac{1}{12}$ th of a second

(D) $\dfrac{1}{20}$ th of a second

29. The Braille code used by the blind people use dot patterns for words. How many dot patterns or characters are used for this code?
(A) 52
(B) 36
(C) 63
(D) 26

30. Nocturnal animals like owl and bat have __________.
(A) large pupil
(B) large cornea
(C) retina with large number of rods
(D) all of these

1.	Ⓐ Ⓑ Ⓒ Ⓓ	7.	Ⓐ Ⓑ Ⓒ Ⓓ	13.	Ⓐ Ⓑ Ⓒ Ⓓ	19	Ⓐ Ⓑ Ⓒ Ⓓ	25.	Ⓐ Ⓑ Ⓒ Ⓓ
2.	Ⓐ Ⓑ Ⓒ Ⓓ	8.	Ⓐ Ⓑ Ⓒ Ⓓ	14.	Ⓐ Ⓑ Ⓒ Ⓓ	20.	Ⓐ Ⓑ Ⓒ Ⓓ	26.	Ⓐ Ⓑ Ⓒ Ⓓ
3.	Ⓐ Ⓑ Ⓒ Ⓓ	9.	Ⓐ Ⓑ Ⓒ Ⓓ	15.	Ⓐ Ⓑ Ⓒ Ⓓ	21.	Ⓐ Ⓑ Ⓒ Ⓓ	27.	Ⓐ Ⓑ Ⓒ Ⓓ
4.	Ⓐ Ⓑ Ⓒ Ⓓ	10.	Ⓐ Ⓑ Ⓒ Ⓓ	16.	Ⓐ Ⓑ Ⓒ Ⓓ	22.	Ⓐ Ⓑ Ⓒ Ⓓ	28.	Ⓐ Ⓑ Ⓒ Ⓓ
5.	Ⓐ Ⓑ Ⓒ Ⓓ	11.	Ⓐ Ⓑ Ⓒ Ⓓ	17.	Ⓐ Ⓑ Ⓒ Ⓓ	23.	Ⓐ Ⓑ Ⓒ Ⓓ	29.	Ⓐ Ⓑ Ⓒ Ⓓ
6.	Ⓐ Ⓑ Ⓒ Ⓓ	12.	Ⓐ Ⓑ Ⓒ Ⓓ	18.	Ⓐ Ⓑ Ⓒ Ⓓ	24.	Ⓐ Ⓑ Ⓒ Ⓓ	30.	Ⓐ Ⓑ Ⓒ Ⓓ

STARS AND THE SOLAR SYSTEM

16

LEARNING OBJECTIVES

➤ The concepts of stars and constellations
➤ Size, shape, features, motion of the moon
➤ The concept of solar system

MULTIPLE CHOICE QUESTIONS

1. The pole star is in the constellation of
   _______.
   (A) Ursa Minor   (B) Orion
   (C) Ursa Major   (D) Scorpius

2. The star nearest to the earth is knows as
   ____.
   (A) proxima centauri (B) Orion
   (C) Sirius   (D) Sun

3. The time taken by a planet to complete
   one revolution is called _______.
   (A) planet day
   (B) planet year
   (C) period of revolution
   (D) period of rotation

4. Planets appear as bright light in the night
   sky because _______.
   (A) they have their own light
   (B) they reflect light from the sun
   (C) they reflect light from nearby planet
   (D) none of these

5. The constellation that resembles a
   'question mark' in the sky is _______.
   (A) Ursa Major   (B) Ursa Minor
   (C) Scorpio   (D) Orion

6. The distance of the star Proxima Centauri
   from the earth is _______.
   (A) 4.3 million km
   (B) 8 1/4 light minutes
   (C) 3 million light years
   (D) 4.3 light years

7. The hottest planet in the solar system is
   _______.
   (A) Mercury   (B) Jupiter
   (C) Venus   (D) Mars

8. Which of the following is a star?
   (A) Diebos
   (B) Orion
   (C) Phobos
   (D) Alpha centauri

9. Asteroids are found between the orbits
   of _______.
   (A) Mercury and Venus
   (B) Mars and Jupiter
   (C) Jupiter and Saturn
   (D) Saturn and Uranus

10. The stone-like object that on entering
    the atmosphere of the earth's surface
    appears as streak of light at night is
    called _______.
    (A) pole star   (B) halley comet
    (C) shooting star   (D) asteroid

11. The sun is located at ________.
    (A) the centre of the solar system
    (B) the centre of the universe
    (C) the centre of the milky way
    (D) none of these
12. The large number of rocks that lie between the orbits of Mars and Jupiter are called ____________.
    (A) comets   (B) meteors
    (C) meteorites   (D) asteroids
13. The constellation in which the stars form the shape of a hunting man is called ________.
    (A) Scorpion   (B) Orion
    (C) Cassiopeia   (D) Ursa major
14. Which of these is called the red planet?
    (A) Venus   (B) Jupiter
    (C) Mars   (D) Saturn
15. Which of these is the largest planet of the solar system?
    (A) Jupiter   (B) Saturn
    (C) Uranus   (D) Venus
16. The largest asteroid in the universe is ________.
    (A) Halley   (B) Ceres
    (C) Orion   (D) Sorpius
17. The first satellite launched by India in March 1975 is ________.
    (A) Bhaskara - I
    (B) INSAT - 2C
    (C) Aryabhata
    (D) Antariksh
18. The earth rotates from west to east about imaginary axis. So, the stars appear to move from ________.
    (A) east to west
    (B) west to east
    (C) north to south
    (D) south to north
19. Stars are classified on the basis of their physical attributes such as ________.
    (A) size
    (B) temperature
    (C) colour and brightness
    (D) all of these
20. The planet having maximum number of moons is ________.
    (A) Saturn
    (B) Venus
    (C) Jupiter
    (D) Uranus
21. We can observe the different phases of moon because ________.
    (A) the shadow of earth falls on the moon
    (B) moon does not reflect sunlight
    (C) of the relative position of the moon, the earth and the sun
    (D) all these
22. How much time does the sunlight take to reach the earth?
    (A) 7.5 minutes
    (B) 7.9 minutes
    (C) 8.3 minutes
    (D) 8.7 minutes
23. For communication network, we need what type of orbit?
    (A) highly elliptical
    (B) geostationary
    (C) polar
    (D) circular
24. Each constellation is made up of different number of stars arranged in different pattern. Orion is one of the constellation. The number of stars of which orion is made up of is _____.
    (A) 5 or 6   (B) 7 or 8
    (C) 9 or 10   (D) 100
25. Which was the first planet to be discovered by the telescope?
    (A) Venus   (B) Pluto
    (C) Saturn   (D) Uranus

26. Which of the following is the name of a constellation?
    i. Great Dear   ii. Little bear
    iii. Hunter
    (A) Only i   (B) Only ii
    (C) Both i and ii   (D) Both ii and iii

27. Find the correct arrangement of the following planets of solar system for their distances from the sun.
    (A) Jupiter < Venus < Saturn < Neptune
    (B) Venus < Jupiter < Saturn < Neptune
    (C) Neptune < Saturn < Jupiter < Venus
    (D) Saturn < Venus < Neptune < Jupiter

28. There are billions of stars in this universe. All of them are at large distance from us. These distances cannot be measured in smaller units, such as, kilometer or meter. It can be measured in light years. What is the distance of nearest stars from the earth?
    (A) 1.5 light years   (B) 2.3 light years
    (C) 3.4 light years   (D) 4.3 light years

29. The planets have their own natural satellites which revolve around the planet in its axis, as the planet revolves around the Sun. The different planets have different number of natural satellites. The number of natural satellites Jupiter has:
    (A) 1   (B) 67
    (C) 17   (D) 28

30. The artificial satellites sent into space in ascending order of their launching date is
    (A) APPLE, EDUSAT, ROHINI, INSAT 4B
    (B) EDUSAT, ROHINI, APPLE, INSAT 4B
    (C) ROHINI, APPLE, EDUSAT, INSAT 4B
    (D) INSAT 4B, EDUSAT, APPLE, ROHINI

Darken Your Choice with HB Pencil

1.	Ⓐ Ⓑ Ⓒ Ⓓ	7.	Ⓐ Ⓑ Ⓒ Ⓓ	13.	Ⓐ Ⓑ Ⓒ Ⓓ	19	Ⓐ Ⓑ Ⓒ Ⓓ	25.	Ⓐ Ⓑ Ⓒ Ⓓ
2.	Ⓐ Ⓑ Ⓒ Ⓓ	8.	Ⓐ Ⓑ Ⓒ Ⓓ	14.	Ⓐ Ⓑ Ⓒ Ⓓ	20.	Ⓐ Ⓑ Ⓒ Ⓓ	26.	Ⓐ Ⓑ Ⓒ Ⓓ
3.	Ⓐ Ⓑ Ⓒ Ⓓ	9.	Ⓐ Ⓑ Ⓒ Ⓓ	15.	Ⓐ Ⓑ Ⓒ Ⓓ	21.	Ⓐ Ⓑ Ⓒ Ⓓ	27.	Ⓐ Ⓑ Ⓒ Ⓓ
4.	Ⓐ Ⓑ Ⓒ Ⓓ	10.	Ⓐ Ⓑ Ⓒ Ⓓ	16.	Ⓐ Ⓑ Ⓒ Ⓓ	22.	Ⓐ Ⓑ Ⓒ Ⓓ	28.	Ⓐ Ⓑ Ⓒ Ⓓ
5.	Ⓐ Ⓑ Ⓒ Ⓓ	11.	Ⓐ Ⓑ Ⓒ Ⓓ	17.	Ⓐ Ⓑ Ⓒ Ⓓ	23.	Ⓐ Ⓑ Ⓒ Ⓓ	29.	Ⓐ Ⓑ Ⓒ Ⓓ
6.	Ⓐ Ⓑ Ⓒ Ⓓ	12.	Ⓐ Ⓑ Ⓒ Ⓓ	18.	Ⓐ Ⓑ Ⓒ Ⓓ	24.	Ⓐ Ⓑ Ⓒ Ⓓ	30.	Ⓐ Ⓑ Ⓒ Ⓓ

POLLUTION OF AIR AND WATER

17

LEARNING OBJECTIVES

- ➤ The concept of pollutant and its types
- ➤ Different types of pollution and its effect on human-health
- ➤ The mechanism of green house effect
- ➤ The adverse effects of acid rain
- ➤ Steps taken to conserve water

MULTIPLE CHOICE QUESTIONS

1. Which of these pollutants causes water pollution?
   (A) sewage
   (B) industrial waste
   (C) fertilizers and pesticides
   (D) all of these

2. Using less water and preventing it from getting polluted is called _________ of water.
   (A) restoration
   (B) preservation
   (C) conservation
   (D) treatment

3. Which of these can cause acid rain?
   (A) CO
   (B) CO_2
   (C) SO_2
   (D) N

4. Which of these processes can not remove germs from water?
   (A) boiling
   (B) filtration through clay pot
   (C) reverse osmosis
   (D) exposure to UV light

5. Chloroflurocarbons damage the _________ layer present in the atmosphere
   (A) Ozone
   (B) Oxygen
   (C) Green
   (D) UV

6. Which of the following gases combines with the blood and prevents it from carrying oxygen to the body?
   (A) CO_2
   (B) NO_2
   (C) CO
   (D) NO_3

7. Which of the following is not a pollutant unless present in excess?
   (A) Sulphur dioxide
   (B) Carbon monoxide
   (C) Nitrogen dioxide
   (D) Carbon dioxide

8. Which of these methods does not result in conservation of water?
   (A) use of drip irrigation
   (B) recycling of water
   (C) cutting vegetation so that less water is lost by transpiration
   (D) planting of trees

9. Water is renewed continuously in nature through _________.
   (A) biological cycle
   (B) water cycle
   (C) nitrogen cycle
   (D) green house effect

10. SPM stands for _________.
    (A) suspended particle mixture
    (B) sand particles matter
    (C) suspended particulate matter
    (D) none of these
11. CFCs are compounds used in _________.
    (A) refrigerators
    (B) air conditioners
    (C) aerosols
    (D) all of these
12. Other than CO_2 which of these contribute towards the green house effect?
    (A) Methane   (B) Nitrous oxide
    (C) Water vapour   (D) All of these
13. Several countries have signed _________ protocol to reduce the emission of green house gases to conserve ozone layer from getting depleted in the atmosphere.
    (A) Kyoto   (B) Tokyo
    (C) Korean   (D) Shanghai
14. Which one of these causes is not a man-made pollution?
    (A) Combustion
    (B) Industrialization
    (C) Dust storm
    (D) Urbanization
15. Which of the following are used in electric water filters to kill all the harmful micro-organisms present in tap water and make it absolutely safe for driving?
    (A) infrared radiation
    (B) gamma radiation
    (C) visible radiation
    (D) ultraviolet radiation
16. Volcanic eruption is a natural cause of air pollution – _________.
    (A) false
    (B) true
    (C) partially false
    (D) none of these

17. Global warming can be reduced by _________.
    (A) minimizing the use of diesel and petrol as fuels
    (B) maximizing the use of LPG, unleaded petrol, ethanol
    (C) planting of more trees and stopping deforestation
    (D) all of these
18. Which of the following will reach the earth in greater amounts if the amount of chloroflouro carbons released into the air increases?
    (A) Infrared rays
    (B) X rays
    (C) Gamma rays
    (D) Ultraviolet rays
19. Which disease can be possible due to drinking of polluted water?
    (A) Cholera   (B) Jaundice
    (C) Typhoid   (D) All of these
20. Corrosion of marble is also called _________.
    (A) marble-disorder
    (B) marble cancer
    (C) marble erosion
    (D) marvelous
21. Which of these gases is present in highest percentage in air?
    (A) Nitrogen   (B) Oxygen
    (C) Carbon dioxide (D) Argon
22. Sculptures/monuments and buildings are destroyed by _________.
    (A) Ozone layer
    (B) Carbon dioxide
    (C) Acid rain
    (D) CFCs
23. Biological pollution in water is caused by _________.
    (A) coal mines
    (B) domestic sewage and animal excreta
    (C) chemical effluents from factories
    (D) oil spills

24. A substance used for disinfecting water
is __________.
   (A) Potassium permanganate
   (B) Coal
   (C) Sodium
   (D) Oxygen

25. The ozone layer in our atmosphere protects us from the harmful effects of ultra violet rays which can cause __________.
   (A) typhoid
   (B) skin disease
   (C) night blindness
   (D) deafness

26. Which of these are the causes of air pollution?
   (A) mining activities
   (B) plant spores
   (C) volcanoes
   (D) all of these

27. Which of these metals is/are found generally in the contaminated water bodies?
   (A) Arsenic and lead
   (B) Cadmium
   (C) Mercury and nickel
   (D) All of these

28. Chlorination of water is done __________.
   (A) to kill all harmful microorganisms
   (B) to remove the odour of water
   (C) to clean the impurities in water
   (D) to make it tasty

29. How are monuments of marble destroyed?
   (A) By sulphur dioxide pollution.
   (B) By carbon monoxide pollution.
   (C) By pesticide pollution.
   (D) By dust particles.

30. Which of these is the major air pollutant in cities like Delhi and Kolkata?
   (A) Carbon monoxide
   (B) Hydrocarbons
   (C) Suspended particulate matter
   (D) Oxides of nitrogen

HOTS (ACHIEVERS SECTION)

31. Which of the following air pollutants is wrongly matched with the effect it causes?
   (A) Dust - reduces photosynthesis in green plants.
   (B) Carbon monoxide - reduces oxygen in the blood.
   (C) Chlorofluorocarbons - damages nerves and tissues.
   (D) Nicotine - hardens and narrows blood vessels.

32. Which of the following does NOT cause air pollution?
   (A) Increasing forest reserves
   (B) Using pesticides in farms
   (C) Developing housing estates
   (D) Quarrying for limestone

33. What is the outcome of the release of carbon particles and smoke from factories?
   (A) Increases the rate of respiration in plants.
   (B) Decreases the rate of photosynthesis in plants.
   (C) Increases the absorption of carbon dioxide by plants.
   (D) Decreases the rate of transpiration in plants.

34. Which of the following gases can result in the formation of acid rain?

(A) Ozone

(B) Carbon monoxide

(C) Sulphur dioxide

(D) Chlorofluorocarbon

35. What is the effect of sulphur dioxide present in air on human beings?

(A) Harms the skin and the lungs

(B) Mixes with the blood and prevents it from carrying oxygen

(C) Affects the heart and the liver

(D) Raises the air temperature

LOGICAL REASONING

LEARNING OBJECTIVES

- ➤ Concept of Alphabetical Order, Alphabetical Quibble and Alphabet series
- ➤ Concept of Odd one out
- ➤ Concept of Coding and Decoding
- ➤ Different directions and their concept
- ➤ Concept behind completion of series and its types
- ➤ Different types of patterns
- ➤ Number test

- ➤ Ranking test
- ➤ Concepts related to analytical reasoning
- ➤ Different types of Venn diagram
- ➤ Concept of embedded figures
- ➤ Concept behind completion of incomplete pattern
- ➤ Water image of letters
- ➤ Water image of numbers
- ➤ Solving the figure matrix questions

MULTIPLE CHOICE QUESTIONS

1. If ZOO stands for 56, DEER stands for 32 then for which numerical value LION stands for?
   - (A) 48
   - (B) 49
   - (C) 50
   - (D) 51

2. If JEANS = 49, COAT = 39 then SHIRT = ?
   - (A) 71
   - (B) 72
   - (C) 73
   - (D) 74

3. If BUD = 27, ROSE = 57 then FLOWER = ?
   - (A) 77
   - (B) 78
   - (C) 79
   - (D) 80

4. BMX, DNW, FOU, ?
   - (A) HQS
   - (B) HPT
   - (C) HPS
   - (D) IPT

5. UPI, SHJ, ODP, MBQ, ?
   - (A) IAW
   - (B) IBV
   - (C) IAV
   - (D) JAW

Direction (6–10): Choose the odd one from the given options.

6. (A) Spanner   (B) Shovel   (C) Spade   (D) Rave
7. (A) Harbour   (B) Island   (C) Coast   (D) Oasis
8. (A) Fibula   (B) Appendix   (C) Pelvis   (D) Vertebra
9. (A) Siachen   (B) Sambhar   (C) Chilka   (D) Bail
10. (A) Optics   (B) Physics   (C) Mechanics   (D) Dynamics

11. In a certain code, HAND is written as SZMW, then what will be the code of MILK?
   - (A) NROP
   - (B) NOPR
   - (C) NORP
   - (D) RNOP

12. In a certain code TURN is written as VWTP, then how is WALK written in that code?
    (A) VCMN
    (B) YCNM
    (C) BMN
    (D) YCON

13. In a coding language GUAVA is coded as HVBWB, then how is JUICE written in that language?
    (A) KVHEF
    (B) KVJDF
    (C) KVIEG
    (D) KUJDT

14. In a certain code JUMP is written as ITLO, then how is ROUND written in that code?
    (A) QMSMB
    (B) QNTMC
    (C) QMTLB
    (D) QNTM

15. If AT = 21; CAT = 24, then what is code for MAT?
    (A) 34
    (B) 35
    (C) 33
    (D) 36

16. Nitesh faces towards North. Turning to his right he walks 20 meters. He then turns to his left and walks 20 meters, then he moves 30 m to his right then turns to his right again and walks 45 meters. At last he turns to his right and moves 35 meters. In which direction is he now from the starting position?
    (A) South
    (B) South-east
    (C) South-west
    (D) North-east

17. Ranjan is looking for Ratan. He went 20 m in the east before turning to his right. He went 20 m before turning to his right again to look Ratan at Mohan's position 30 m from this point. Ratan was not there. From that point he went 100 m to his north before meeting Ratan. At what distance did Ranjan meet Ratan from the starting point?
    (A) 60 m
    (B) 80 m
    (C) 100 m
    (D) 120 m

18. Dinesh walks 10 m in front and 10 m to the right then turning to his left three times he walks 5 m, 15 m, 15 m respectively. How far is he from his starting position?
    (A) 5 m
    (B) 10 m
    (C) 15 m
    (D) None of these

19. Pritam walks 15 m towards south then turning to his right he walks 30 m then turning to his left he walks 20 m. Again he turns to his left and walks 30 m. How far is he from his starting position?
    (A) 25 m
    (B) 35 m
    (C) 45 m
    (D) 55 m

20. Ankit is facing East. He turns 100° in the clockwise direction and then 145° in the anti-clockwise direction. In which direction is he facing now?
    (A) North-east
    (B) East
    (C) North-west
    (D) South-west

Direction: Find the next term in the following series.

21. 6, 15, 28, 45, 66, ……?
    (A) 91
    (B) 92
    (C) 93
    (D) 94

22. 12, 19, 28, 39, 52, ?
    (A) 65
    (B) 66
    (C) 67
    (D) 68

23. 10, 22, 46, 94, ?
    (A) 189
    (B) 190
    (C) 191
    (D) 192

24. 15, 31, 63, 127, 255, ?
    (A) 508
    (B) 510
    (C) 511
    (D) 512

25. 40320, 5760, 960, 192, 48, ……?
    (A) 14
    (B) 16
    (C) 18
    (D) 22

Directions (26–30): Observe the given pattern and choose the correct option.

26. 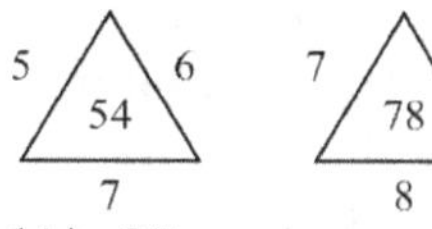
    (A) 85
    (B) 86
    (C) 87
    (D) 89

27. 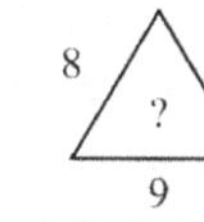
    (A) 11
    (B) 12
    (C) 13
    (D) 14

28. 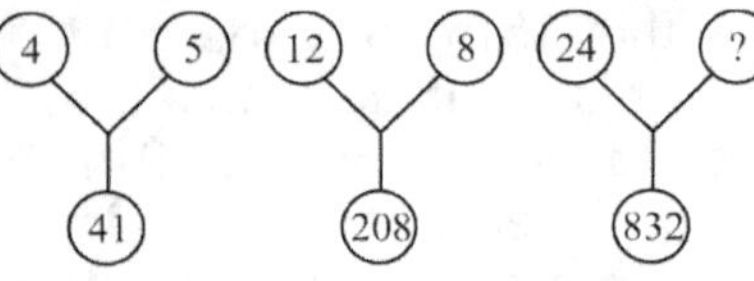

(A) 14   (B) 16
(C) 18   (D) 20

29. 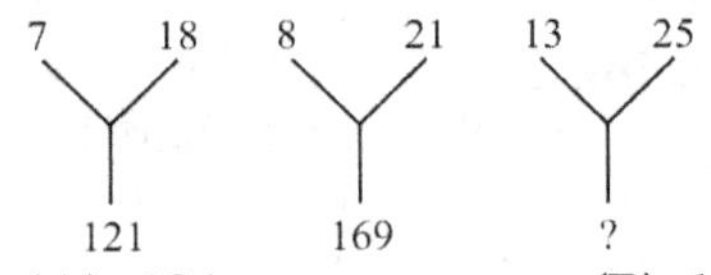

(A) 121   (B) 144
(C) 169   (D) 196

30. 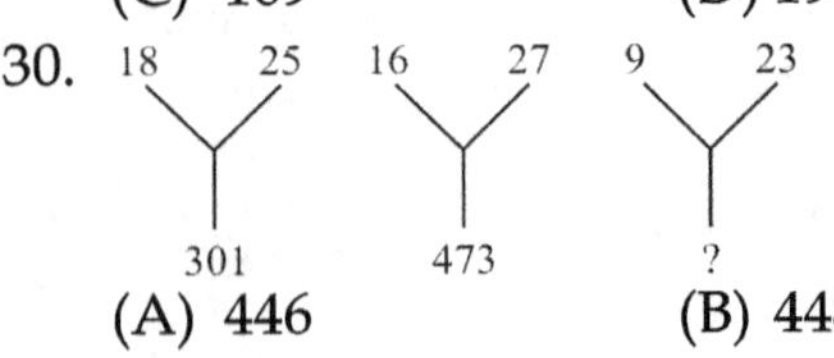

(A) 446   (B) 448
(C) 456   (D) 458

31. How many odd numbers are there in the sequence each of which is immediately followed by an odd number?

5 1 4 7 3 9 8 5 7 2 6 3 1 5 8 6 3 8 5 2 2 4 3 4 9 6

(A) 3   (B) 5
(C) 6   (D) 4

32. How many odd numbers are there in the sequence which are immediately preceded and also immediately followed by an even number in the sequence?

5 1 4 7 3 2 5 6 8 9 6 7 3 2 1 5 6 4 3 2 7 4

(A) 4   (B) 3
(C) 5   (D) 2

33. How many even numbers are there which are immediately followed by an odd number and also immediately preceded by an odd number in the sequence?

8 4 7 6 5 3 2 5 1 6 4 3 2 6 7 9 8 5

(A) 3   (B) 4
(C) 2   (D) 15

34. In the series

2 5 3 4 8 7 4 2 6 7 1 5 8 3 7 4 5 3

How many pairs of successive numbers have a difference of 3?

(A) 3   (B) 4
(C) 2   (D) 5

35. How many 5's are there in the sequence which are immediately preceded by 4 and immediately followed by 7?

2 3 4 5 6 1 4 5 7 1 2 4 5 7 3 8 4 5 9 6 5 3

(A) 1   (B) 2
(C) 3   (D) 4

Directions (36–40): In each of the following problems, find the number of triangles in the given figure:

36. 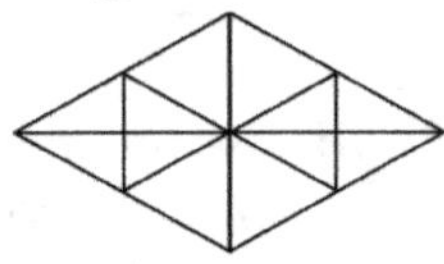

(A) 22   (B) 24
(C) 28   (D) 32

37. 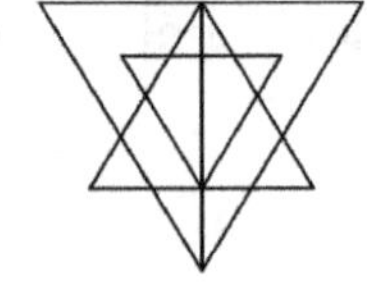

(A) 22   (B) 23
(C) 25   (D) 27

38. 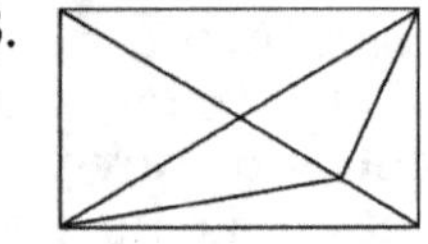

(A) 14   (B) 15
(C) 16   (D) 17

39. 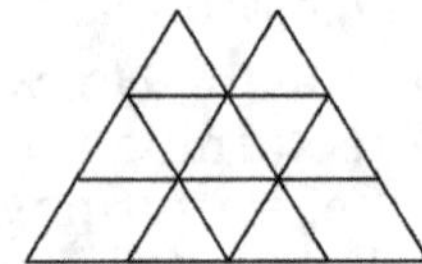

(A) 16   (B) 17
(C) 18   (D) 22

40. 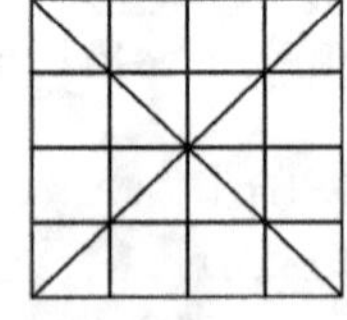

(A) 48   (B) 46
(C) 52   (D) 56

Directions (41–44): In the given figure, there are three intersecting circles each representing certain section of people.

Different regions are marked p, d, r, s, t, u, v. Read the statement in the given question and choose the letter of the region which correctly represents the statement.

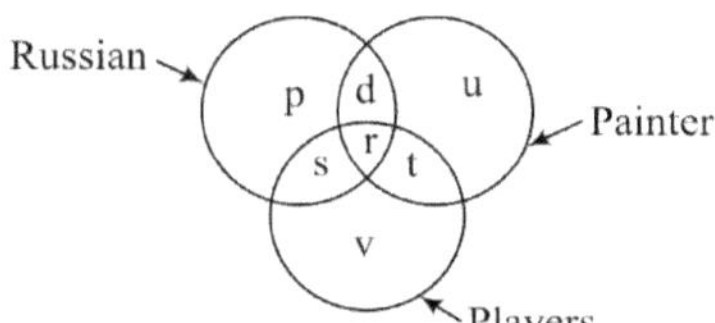

41. Russian who are painters but not players
   (A) d
   (B) t
   (C) s
   (D) v

42. Russian who are painters as well as players
   (A) p
   (B) d
   (C) r
   (D) s

43. Russian who are players but not painters
   (A) p
   (B) d
   (C) r
   (D) s

44. Painters who are neither Russian nor players
   (A) d
   (B) r
   (C) u
   (D) t

Directions (45–49): In each of the following questions, fig. (X) is embedded in any one of the four alterative figures (A), (B), (C) or (D). Find the alternative which contains fig. (X) as its part.

45.
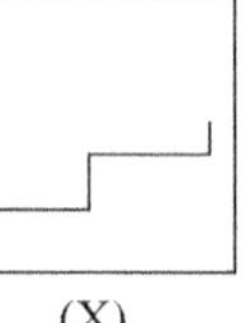
(X)
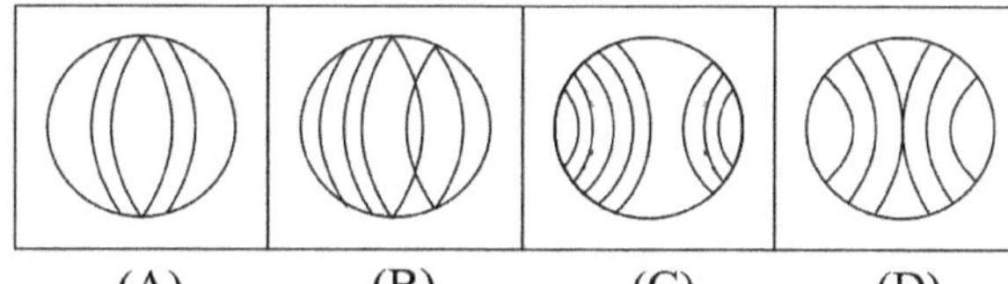
(A)   (B)   (C)   (D)

46.
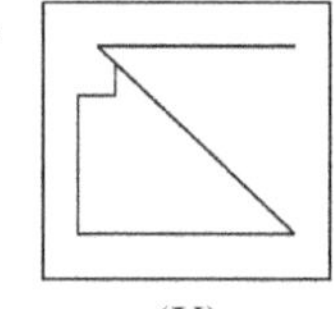
(X)
(A)   (B)   (C)   (D)

47.
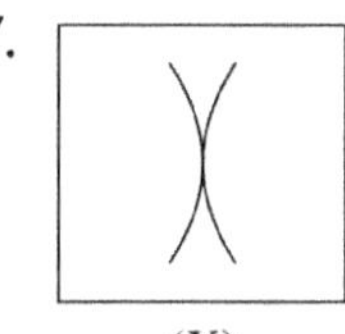
(X)
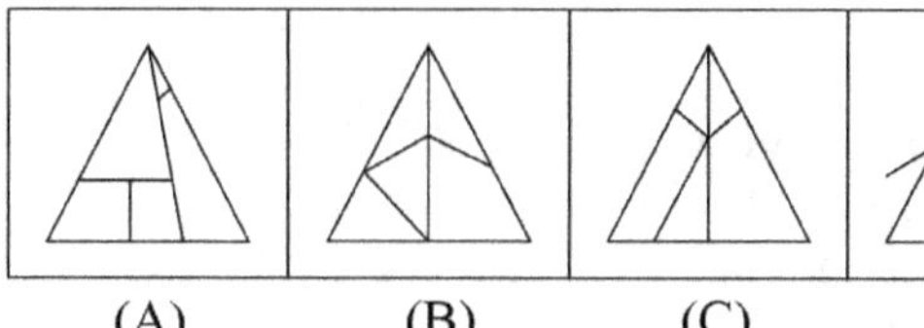
(A)   (B)   (C)   (D)

48.
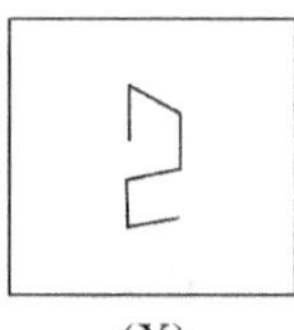
(X)
(A)   (B)   (C)   (D)

49.
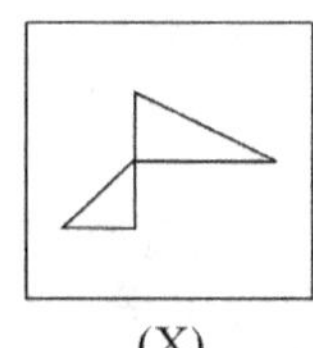
(X)
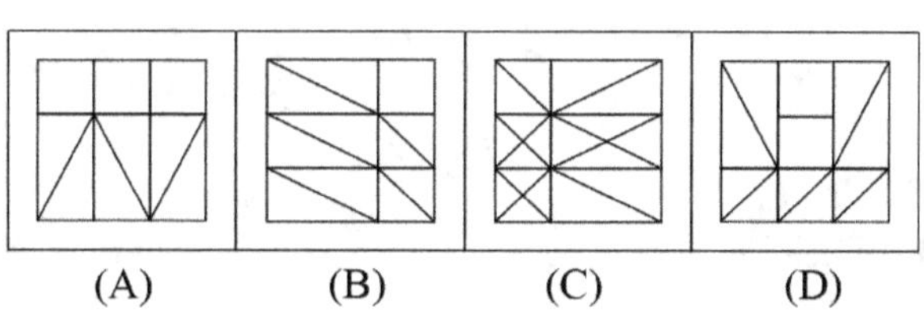
(A)   (B)   (C)   (D)

Directions (50 – 54): In the following problems, select a figure from amongst the four options which when placed in the blank space of figure (X) would complete the pattern.

50. 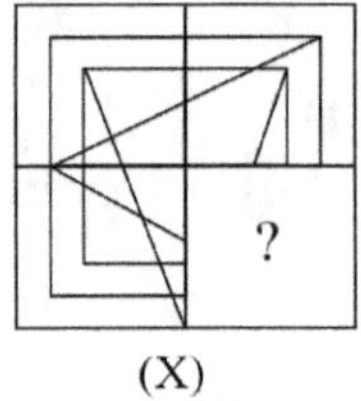

(X)   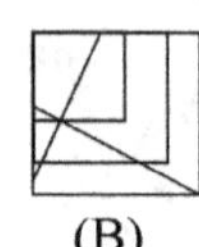 (A)   (B)   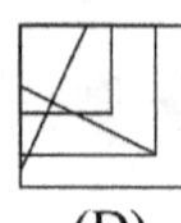 (C)   (D)

51. 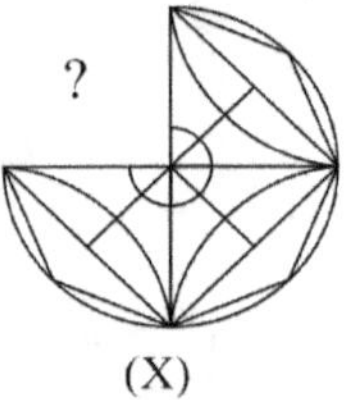

(X)    (A)   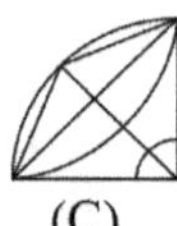 (B)    (C)   (D)

52. 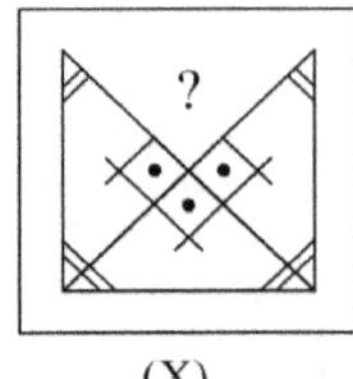

(X)   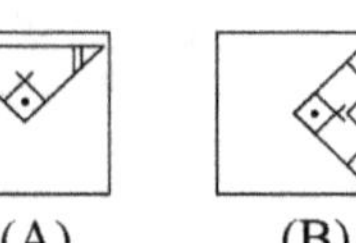 (A)   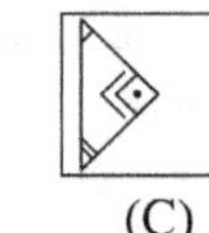 (B)   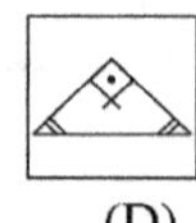 (C)   (D)

53. 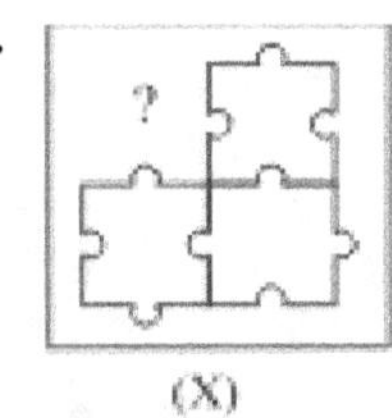

(X)   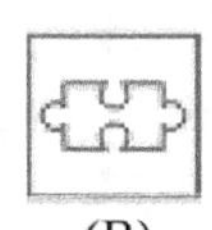 (A)    (B)    (C)   (D)

54. 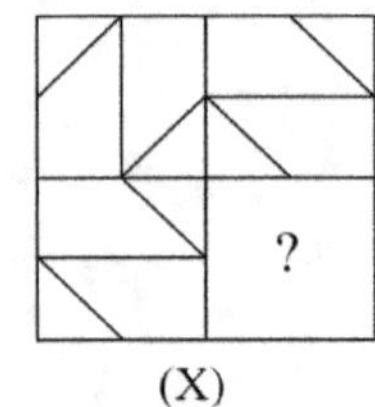

(X)   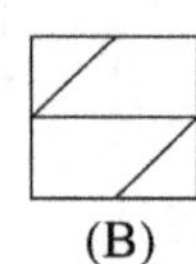 (A)   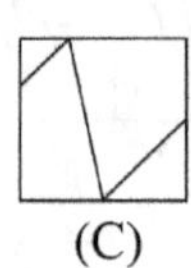 (B)   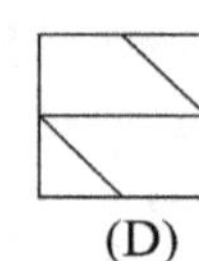 (C)   (D)

Directions (55 – 59): In each of the following questions, you are given a combination of alphabets and/or numbers followed by four alternatives (A), (B), (C) and (D). Choose the alternative which most closely resembles the water image of the given combination.

55. DISC
(A) CSID   (B) ƆSIɑ
(C) DIƧC   (D) DISC

56. FROG
(A) ʀᴏɢ   (B) GORF
(C) Ϝᴿᴼᴳ   (D) Ϝᴿᴼᴳ

57. RECRUIT
(A) ᴿᴱᴄ ᴿᴜᴵᵀ   (B) ʀᴇᴄʀᴜɪᴛ
(C) RECRUIT   (D) ᴛᴵᴜᴿᴄᴱʀ

58. ACOUSTIC
(A) ᴬᴄᴼᴜꙅᵀᴵᴄ   (B) ᴬᴄᴼᴜꙅᵀᴵᴄ
(C) ᴬᴄᴼᴜꙅᵀᴵᴄ   (D) ᴬᴄᴼᴜꙅ ᵀᴵᴄ

59. FAMILY
    (A) ᖴᗅᗰIᒪY   (B) ᖴᗅᗰIᒪY
    (C) FAMILY   (D) FAMILY

Directions: In the following questions, study the given matrix, and find the correct option for the question mark from the given four options.

60.
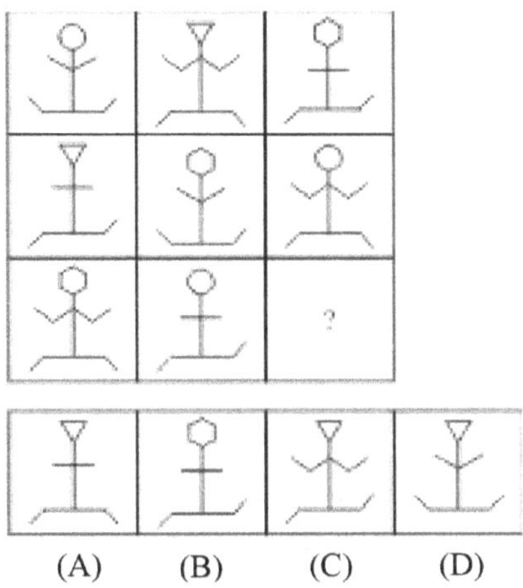

(A)   (B)   (C)   (D)

61.
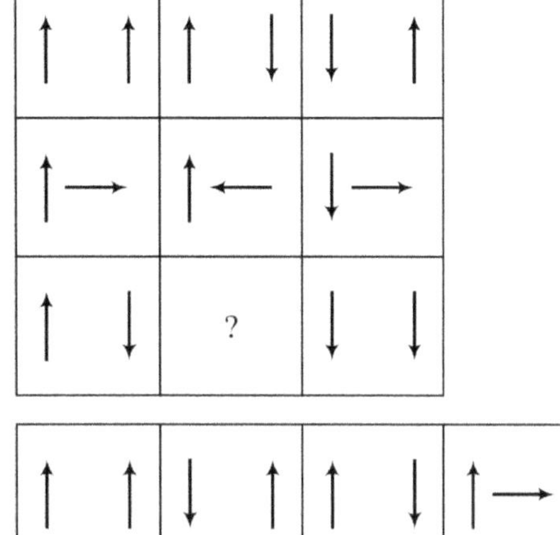

(A)   (B)   (C)   (D)

62.
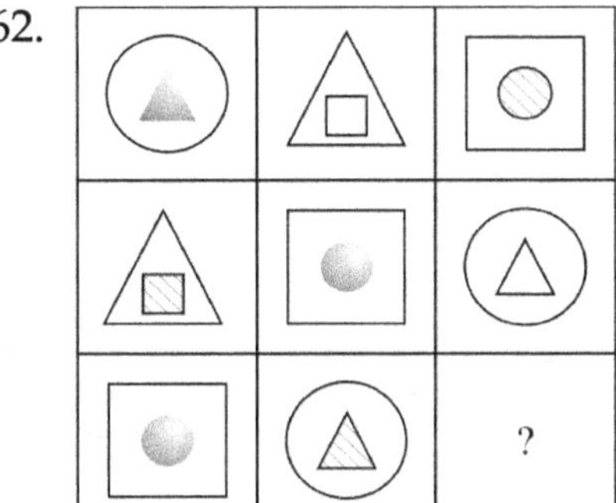

(A)   (B)   (C)   (D)

63.
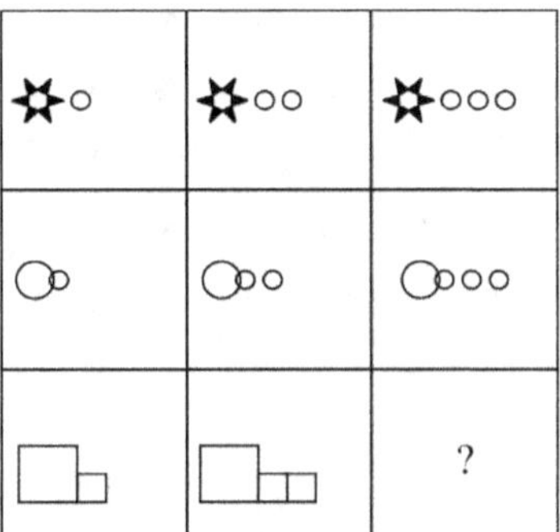

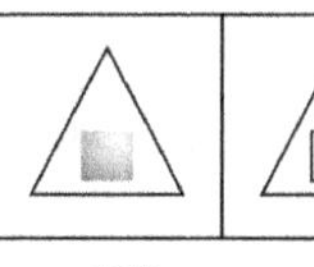

(A)   (B)   (C)   (D)

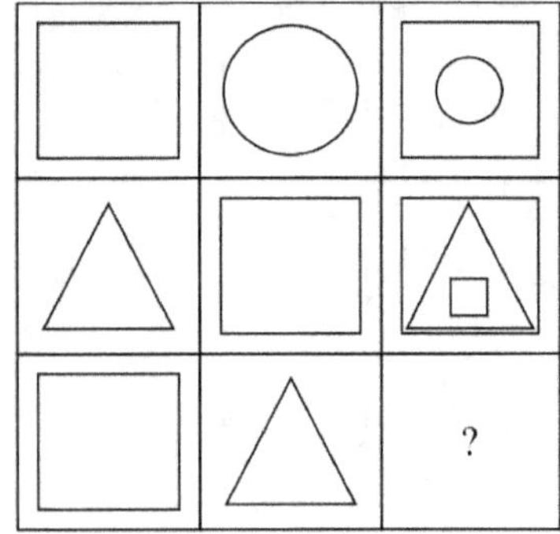
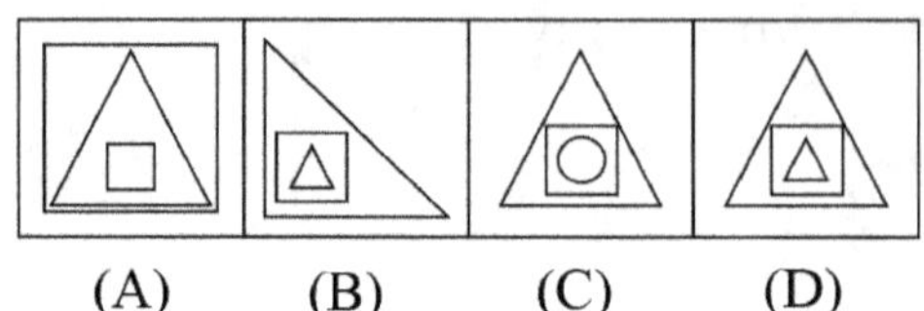
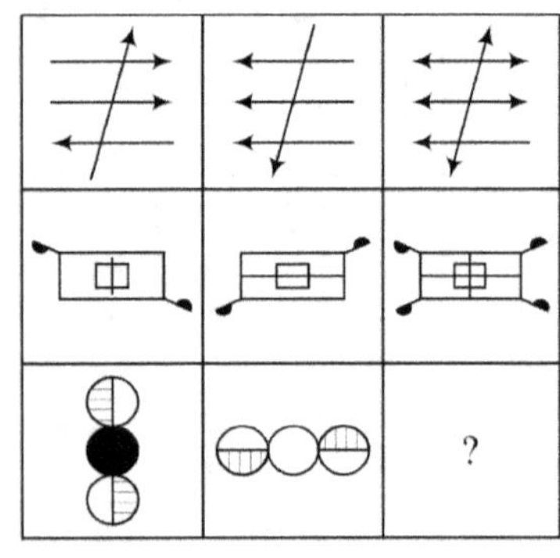
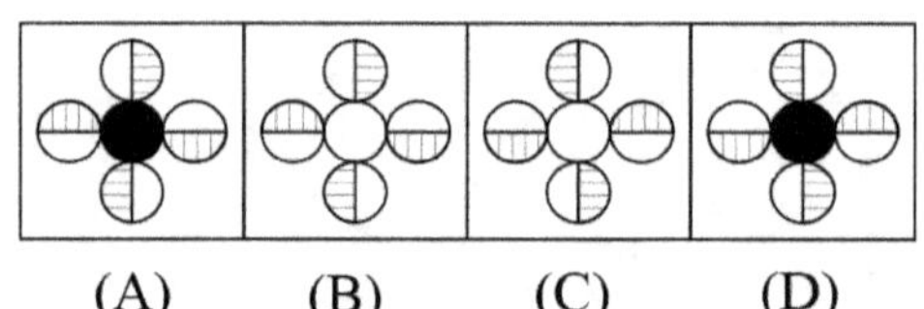

Darken Your Choice with HB Pencil

1.	Ⓐ Ⓑ Ⓒ Ⓓ	14.	Ⓐ Ⓑ Ⓒ Ⓓ	27.	Ⓐ Ⓑ Ⓒ Ⓓ	40.	Ⓐ Ⓑ Ⓒ Ⓓ	53	Ⓐ Ⓑ Ⓒ Ⓓ
2.	Ⓐ Ⓑ Ⓒ Ⓓ	15.	Ⓐ Ⓑ Ⓒ Ⓓ	28.	Ⓐ Ⓑ Ⓒ Ⓓ	41.	Ⓐ Ⓑ Ⓒ Ⓓ	54.	Ⓐ Ⓑ Ⓒ Ⓓ
3.	Ⓐ Ⓑ Ⓒ Ⓓ	16.	Ⓐ Ⓑ Ⓒ Ⓓ	29.	Ⓐ Ⓑ Ⓒ Ⓓ	42.	Ⓐ Ⓑ Ⓒ Ⓓ	55.	Ⓐ Ⓑ Ⓒ Ⓓ
4.	Ⓐ Ⓑ Ⓒ Ⓓ	17.	Ⓐ Ⓑ Ⓒ Ⓓ	30.	Ⓐ Ⓑ Ⓒ Ⓓ	43.	Ⓐ Ⓑ Ⓒ Ⓓ	56.	Ⓐ Ⓑ Ⓒ Ⓓ
5.	Ⓐ Ⓑ Ⓒ Ⓓ	18.	Ⓐ Ⓑ Ⓒ Ⓓ	31.	Ⓐ Ⓑ Ⓒ Ⓓ	44.	Ⓐ Ⓑ Ⓒ Ⓓ	57.	Ⓐ Ⓑ Ⓒ Ⓓ
6.	Ⓐ Ⓑ Ⓒ Ⓓ	19.	Ⓐ Ⓑ Ⓒ Ⓓ	32.	Ⓐ Ⓑ Ⓒ Ⓓ	45.	Ⓐ Ⓑ Ⓒ Ⓓ	58.	Ⓐ Ⓑ Ⓒ Ⓓ
7.	Ⓐ Ⓑ Ⓒ Ⓓ	20.	Ⓐ Ⓑ Ⓒ Ⓓ	33.	Ⓐ Ⓑ Ⓒ Ⓓ	46.	Ⓐ Ⓑ Ⓒ Ⓓ	59.	Ⓐ Ⓑ Ⓒ Ⓓ
8.	Ⓐ Ⓑ Ⓒ Ⓓ	21.	Ⓐ Ⓑ Ⓒ Ⓓ	34.	Ⓐ Ⓑ Ⓒ Ⓓ	47.	Ⓐ Ⓑ Ⓒ Ⓓ	60.	Ⓐ Ⓑ Ⓒ Ⓓ
9.	Ⓐ Ⓑ Ⓒ Ⓓ	22.	Ⓐ Ⓑ Ⓒ Ⓓ	35.	Ⓐ Ⓑ Ⓒ Ⓓ	48.	Ⓐ Ⓑ Ⓒ Ⓓ	61.	Ⓐ Ⓑ Ⓒ Ⓓ
10.	Ⓐ Ⓑ Ⓒ Ⓓ	23.	Ⓐ Ⓑ Ⓒ Ⓓ	36.	Ⓐ Ⓑ Ⓒ Ⓓ	49	Ⓐ Ⓑ Ⓒ Ⓓ	62.	Ⓐ Ⓑ Ⓒ Ⓓ
11.	Ⓐ Ⓑ Ⓒ Ⓓ	24.	Ⓐ Ⓑ Ⓒ Ⓓ	37.	Ⓐ Ⓑ Ⓒ Ⓓ	50.	Ⓐ Ⓑ Ⓒ Ⓓ	63.	Ⓐ Ⓑ Ⓒ Ⓓ
12.	Ⓐ Ⓑ Ⓒ Ⓓ	25.	Ⓐ Ⓑ Ⓒ Ⓓ	38.	Ⓐ Ⓑ Ⓒ Ⓓ	51.	Ⓐ Ⓑ Ⓒ Ⓓ	64.	Ⓐ Ⓑ Ⓒ Ⓓ
13.	Ⓐ Ⓑ Ⓒ Ⓓ	26.	Ⓐ Ⓑ Ⓒ Ⓓ	39.	Ⓐ Ⓑ Ⓒ Ⓓ	52.	Ⓐ Ⓑ Ⓒ Ⓓ	65.	Ⓐ Ⓑ Ⓒ Ⓓ

OLYMPIAD WORKBOOK (NSO) CLASS – 8

MODEL TEST PAPER

1. If each vowel in the word MOUNTAIN is replaced by the next letter in the English alphabet and each consonant is replaced by the previous letter in the English alphabet, then which of the following will be the fourth letter to the left of seventh letter from the left end?

   (A) T (B) V
   (C) N (D) P

2. Study the following arrangement carefully and answer the question given below.

   B A 5 D % R I * F H 6 # V 9 $ 3 E 7 G 1 ÷ 2 M K X 8 U F W Z N

   What should come in place of the (?) in the following series based on the above arrangement?

   ADIF69   37÷ ?

   (A) 2KU (B) MXU
   (C) MXF (D) XUM

3. Two rows of numbers are given. The resultant number in each row is to be worked out separately based on the following rules. The operations on numbers progress from left to right. Rules :

   (i) If a two-digit odd number is followed by a prime number, the first number is to be multiplied by the prime number.

   (ii) If an even number is followed by another even number, the first number is to be divided by the second number.

   (iii) If an odd number is followed by a composite odd number, the first number is to be added to the second number.

   (iv) If an even number which is a multiple of 5 is followed by another number which is again a multiple of 5, the second number is to be subtracted from the first number.

   (v) If a number which is a perfect square is followed by another number which is also a perfect square, then the square roots of the two numbers is to be multiplied.

   64   25   25
   88   8   n

   If n is the resultant of the first row, what is the resultant of the second row?

   (A) 24 (B) 36
   (C) 28 (D) 26

4. P, Q, R, S, T, V and W are sitting around a circle facing the centre. R is third to the right of V, who is second to the right of P. T is second to the left of Q, who is second to the left of W. V is sitting between S and W. Who is sitting between T and V?

   (A) W
   (B) R
   (C) S
   (D) Can't be determined

5. Read the following information carefully.
   'A*B' means 'A multiplied by B'.
   'A@B' means 'A minus B'.
   'A $B' means 'A plus B'.
   'A #B' means 'A divided by B'.

Mohit donates 7% of his monthly salary R to charity and spends Rs. 3,000 per month on his house rent. What is the amount left with him out of his monthly salary after excluding house rent and charity amount?

(A) R @ (3000 @ 7 * 100#R)

(B) R @ (7 * R # 100 @ 3000)

(C) R @ (R * 7 # 100 $ 3000)

(D) None of these

6. Study the given information carefully and answer the question that follows.

■ P, Q, R, S, T, U and V are sitting in a row facing North.

■ T is to the immediate right of V.

■ P is the neighbour of R and U.

■ V is 4th to the right of Q.

■ Person who is third to the left of U is at one of the ends.

Who is second to the right of U?

(A) T
(B) V
(C) S
(D) P

7. In a certain code language, if 'TUTORIAL' is written as 'WRWLUFDI', then how will 'GUIDANCE' be written in that language?

(A) HFQDGLXJ
(B) FGPLKYJZ
(C) JRLADFKB
(D) JRLADKFB

8. How many pair of letters are there in the word OPERATION which have as many letters between them in the word as in the English alphabet?

(A) Five

(B) Six

(C) Seven

(D) More than seven

9. Priyanshu walked 8 m in East, then he turned right and walked 3 m. Again he turned to the right and walked 12 m. How far is he now from the starting point?

(A) 20 m
(B) 4 m
(C) 5 m
(D) 23 m

10. How many 8's are there in the given series, which are immediately preceded by a number which does not divide it but followed by a number which divides it?

4 8 2 8 2 8 3 8 5 8 8 5 3 2 8 2 3 8 4 7 1 5 8 3 8 2 8 6 8 8 6

(A) 1
(B) 2
(C) 3
(D) 4

11. A box is being pushed horizontally along a rough surface and a constant acceleration is achieved. If the push is stopped, the box will

(A) Slow down and finally stop

(B) Continue to move at constant speed

(C) Continue to accelerate at a lower rate

(D) Stop immediately.

12. A block of mass 4 kg and dimensions 10 cm × 20 cm × 30 cm rests on the floor. If $g = 10$ ms^{-2}, then the maximum pressure the block can exert on the floor is

(A) 2000 N m^{-2}
(B) 1000 N m^{-2}
(C) 4000 N m^{-2}
(D) 1333 N m^{-2}

13. Which of the following statements are true about both light and sound?

(i) They are forms of energy.

(ii) They can be converted into other forms of energy.

(iii) They undergo reflection.

(A) (i) and (ii) only

(B) (ii) and (iii) only

(C) (i) and (iii) only

(D) (i), (ii) and (iii)

14. Which of the following options correctly represents the relative positions of the Sun (S), Moon (M) and Earth (E) on the day of full moon and new moon?

	Full Moon	New Moon
(A)	MES	MSE
(B)	SME	ESM
(C)	SEM	SME
(D)	ESM	EMS

15. What is the use of cooking oil in frying a fish in terms of heat transfer?
   (A) To increase rate of heat transfer to the fish via radiation.
   (B) To increase rate of heat transfer to the fish via convection.
   (C) To increase rate of heat transfer to the fish via conduction.
   (D) To increase rate of heat transfer to the fish via evaporation.

16. Why does a horse need to pull harder during the first few steps in pulling the cart?
   (A) Static friction is greater than sliding friction.
   (B) Sliding friction is greater than rolling friction.
   (C) No frictional force acts after the cart comes in motion.
   (D) Air friction is greater during first few steps of motion.

17. Which of the following statements are correct?
   (i) Venus is the hottest planet of the solar system.
   (ii) Jupiter is called the red planet as it has a large red spot on its surface.
   (iii) Revolving speed of Mercury is fastest of all planets.
   (iv) Mars has no natural satellites of its own.
   (v) Saturn is the least dense planet among all planets.
   (A) (ii) and (iii) only
   (B) (ii), (iv) and (v) only
   (C) (i), (iii) and (v) only
   (D) (i), (ii), (iv) and (v) only

18. The intensity of sound wave gets reduced by 10% on passing through a slab. The total reduction in intensity on passing through three consecutive slabs is
   (A) 30% (B) 70%
   (C) 27.1% (D) 72.9%

19. Read the given statements and select the correct option.

   Statement 1 : Smoke goes upwards.

   Statement 2 : The warm air is lighter than the cold air.
   (A) Both statements 1 and 2 are true and statement 2 is the correct explanation of statement 1.
   (B) Both statements 1 and 2 are true but statement 2 is not the correct explanation of statement 1.
   (C) Statement 1 is true but statement 2 is false.
   (D) Both statements 1 and 2 are false.

20. Fill in the blanks by choosing an appropriate option.

   Acids are compounds that contain (i) atoms. Sulphuric acid is one such example which is a (ii) acid. It is neutralised by alkalies and forms salts called (iii) . Acids react with metals to give (iv) gas.

	(i)	(ii)	(iii)	(iv)
(A)	Hydrogen	Weak	Sulphites	Oxygen
(B)	Oxygen	Weak	Sulphates	Hydrogen
(C)	Hydrogen	Strong	Sulphites	Oxygen
(D)	Hydrogen	Strong	Sulphates	Hydrogen

21. Which of the following statements are true?
   I.   In the luminous zone of candle flame, vaporised wax gets oxidised to carbon dioxide which burns with a blue flame.
   II. There is no burning in the dark inner zone of the flame.
   III. Non luminous zone is the hottest part of the flame.
   IV. Luminous zone of a f lame is mainly due to incomplete burning of carbon.
   (A) I and III only
   (B) II and III only
   (C) II, III and IV only
   (D) All of these

22. Read the given paragraph with few blanks and select the option that correctly fills up any 3 of these.

   (i) is the ability to blend with the surroundings. It is protective to prey insects like (ii) and also advantageous to predators like (iii). (iv) is the resemblance of one species with another. The species which is imitated is called (v) while the species which imitates is called (vi).
   (A) (i) Mimicry, (iv) Camouflage, (vi) Mimic
   (B) (ii) Leaf insect, (iv) Mimicry, (v) Model
   (C) (i) Camouflage, (iii) Praying mantis, (vi) Model
   (D) (ii) Grasshopper, (iii) Stick insect, (v) Mimic

23. Read the following statements and select the correct option.
   (A) A daughter receives X-chromosome from her mother only.
   (B) Human beings possess 22 pairs of autosomes and 1 pair of sex chromosomes.
   (C) A new human individual develops from a cell called gamete only.
   (D) Pituitary gland produces thyroxine.

24. A 20 Pa pressure is applied on the head of a nail placed perpendicular to the surface of a wall. If the area of cross-section of the tip of the nail is (1/10) times the area of cross-section of the head, the pressure exerted at the wall is
   (A) 10 Pa
   (B) 20 Pa
   (C) 200 Pa
   (D) None of these

25. A fire can be made by rubbing two objects together such as rubbing two pieces of rock having rough surfaces. Which of the following statements explain why a fire can be made by rubbing two objects together?
   (i)   Friction slows down moving objects.
   (ii) Fire gives out heat and light energy.
   (iii) Friction produces heat.
   (iv) Fire has no mass.
   (A) (ii) only
   (B) (iii) only
   (C) (i), (ii) and (iii) only
   (D) (ii) and (iv) only

26. In the given figure, two mirrors X and Y are situated at an angle of 60° with each other and a ray of light is incident on mirror X at an angle of 50°. When the ray is reflected by the mirror Y, then what is angle of reflection at this mirror?

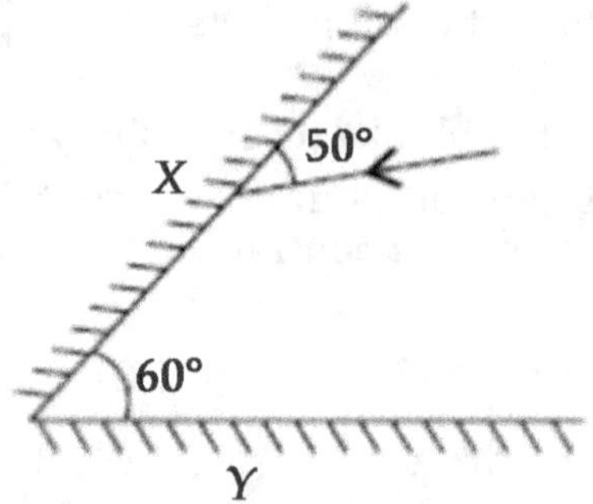

   (A) 35°
   (B) 55°
   (C) 50°
   (D) 20°

27. The device used to prevent the flow of excess current in the circuit is
   (A) Switch
   (B) Fuse
   (C) Bulb
   (D) Coil

OLYMPIAD WORKBOOK (NSO) CLASS – 8

28. Read the given statements and select the correct option.

Statement 1: The seasons are caused by the tilt of Earth's axis.

Statement 2: The axis of Earth is tilted at an angle of 23 (1°/2) to the plane of its orbit.

(A) Both statements 1 and 2 are true and statement 2 is the correct explanation of statement 1.

(B) Both statements 1 and 2 are true but statement 2 is not the correct explanation of statement 1.

(C) Statement 1 is true but statement 2 is false.

(D) Statement 1 is false but statement 2 is true.

29. Fill in the blanks by choosing an appropriate option.

The loudness of sound depends on its ___(i)___. The ___(ii)___ determines the pitch of a sound. A bird makes a ___(iii)___ sound where as a lion makes a ___(iv)___ sound. Usually voice of a woman has a ___(v)___ frequency than that of a man.

	(i)	(ii)	(iii)	(iv)	(v)
(A)	Amplitude	Frequency	Low-pitched	High-pitched	Lower
(B)	Pitch	Frequency	Low-pitched	High-pitched	Lower
(C)	Amplitude	Frequency	High-pitched	Low-pitched	Higher
(D)	Frequency	Pitch	High-pitched	Low-pitched	Higher

30. Read the given statements and select the correct option.

Statement 1: It takes a much longer time and covers more distance to stop a moving ship in water than a moving car with same speed on the road.

Statement 2: The friction on water surface is much less than the solid surface.

(A) Both statements 1 and 2 are true and statement 2 is the correct explanation of statement 1.

(B) Both statements 1 and 2 are true but statement 2 is not the correct explanation of statement 1.

(C) Statement 1 is true but statement 2 is false.

(D) Statement 1 is false but statement 2 is true.

31. Which of the following statements is/are always true regarding a converging lens?

I. When the object is placed nearer to the focal point, the image gets bigger.

II. When the object is placed away from the lens, image gets smaller.

III. When the object is placed very far away from the lens, the image distance approaches focal length.

(A) I and II only (B) II and III only

(C) I and III only (D) II only

32. Which one of the following is a right arrangement?

(A) Rolling friction > static friction > sliding friction

(B) Sliding friction < static friction < rolling friction

(C) Rolling friction > static friction < sliding friction

(A) Static friction > sliding friction > rolling friction

33. The force that is responsible for revolution of the earth around the sun is

(A) Electric force

(B) Magnetic force

(C) Electromagnetic force

(D) Gravitational force

34. A plane mirror forms a virtual image. The distance between Mahima and her image in a plane mirror is 10 m. How much distance should she move in order to get the distance of 5 m between herself and her image?
(A) 2.5 m away from the mirror
(B) 2.5 m towards the mirror
(C) 5 m away from the mirror
(D) 5 m towards the mirror

35. Read the given statements and select the correct option.

Statement 1: When an object is placed between two plane parallel mirrors, then all the images formed are of unequal intensity.

Statement 2: In case of plane parallel mirrors, only two images are possible.
(A) Both statements 1 and 2 are true and statement 2 is the correct explanation of statement 1.
(B) Both statements 1 and 2 are true but statement 2 is not the correct explanation of statement 1.
(C) Statement 1 is true and statement 2 is false.
(D) Both statements 1 and 2 are false.

36. Which coil produces the strongest electromagnet for a given flow of current?
(A) A 10 cm coil with 100 turns
(B) A 5 cm coil with 200 turns
(C) A 10 cm coil with 200 turns
(D) A 20 cm coil with 200 turns

37. While drinking a soft drink with the help of a straw, the pressure in the straw is _______ and the pressure in the bottle is _______.
(A) High, less   (B) High, high
(C) Less, less   (D) Less, high

38. Which of the following statements is incorrect?
(A) Gold and silver are the most malleable and ductile metals.
(B) All metals are hard and strong.

(C) Mercury and gallium are metals which exist in liquid state at room temperature.
(D) Most of the metals have high specific gravities.

39. Following statements are given by four students:

Rashmi: Sodium chloride is an acidic salt whereas washing soda is a basic salt.

Akshi: The aqueous solution of sugar does not change the colour of either red litmus solution or blue litmus solution.

Reema: Tamarind tastes sour whereas baking soda is bitter in taste.

Shristi: Apple juice does not change the colour of red litmus solution.

The incorrect statement(s) is/are given by
(A) Reema and Shristi only
(B) Rashmi only
(C) Akshi and Reema only
(D) Akshi and Shristi only

40. Read the given statements and select the correct option.

Statement 1: Bakelite is used for making electric switches and plugs.

Statement 2: It is a thermosetting polymer and an insulator.
(A) Both statements 1 and 2 are true and statement 2 is the correct explanation of statement 1.
(B) Both statements 1 and 2 are true but statement 2 is not the correct explanation of statement 1.
(C) Statement 1 is true but statement 2 is false.
(D) Both statements 1 and 2 are false.

41. Which of the following statements is/are incorrect?
(i) Perspex is thermoplastic which is transparent like glass but is much stronger.
(ii) Nylon thread cannot support more weight as compared to steel wire of same dimensions.

(iii) Polyester and nylon on burning give smell of burning hair.

(iv) Terylene, a synthetic fibre, can be used instead of wool.

(A) II, III and IV only

(B) II and IV only

(C) I only

(D) I, II, III and IV

42. Given below is a list of few chemicals that are used for protection of crops.

(i) Dalapon   (ii) Butachlor

(iii) Malathion   (iv) Simazine

(v) Disyston   (vi) Gammexane

How many of these are used as insecticides?

(A) 3   (B) 4

(C) 2   (D) 5

43. Select the incorrect statement.

(i) Sulphur dioxide gas combines with haemoglobin of blood and prevents transport of oxygen by it.

(ii) Methane, nitrous oxide and water vapour present in atmospheric air contribute to global warming.

(iii) Lead emitted by automobile exhaust could cause brain damage.

(iv) Oxides of sulphur and nitrogen present in air could affect lungs.

(A) I only   (B) I and IV only

(C) I, II and IV only   (D) I and III only

44. Refer to the given diagram:

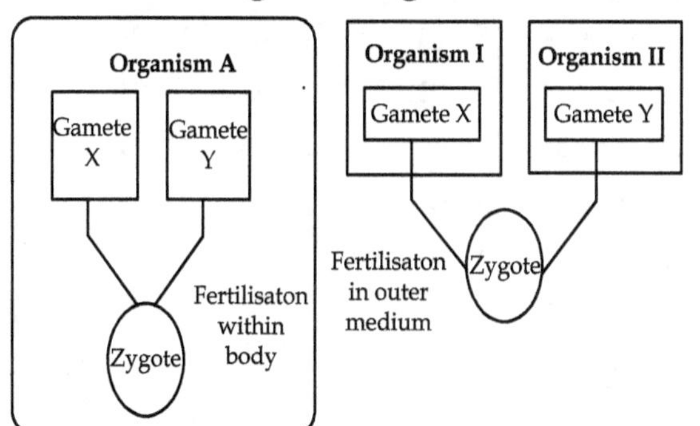

Select the correct option regarding this:

(A) Organism A is hermaphrodite or bisexual and may undergo either self or cross fertilisation.

(B) Organisms I and II are unisexual and exhibit external fertilisation.

(C) Organism A could be Taenia if it undergoes self fertilisation or it could be earthworm if it undergoes cross fertilisation.

(D) All of these

45. Refer to the given figure and select the incorrect option.

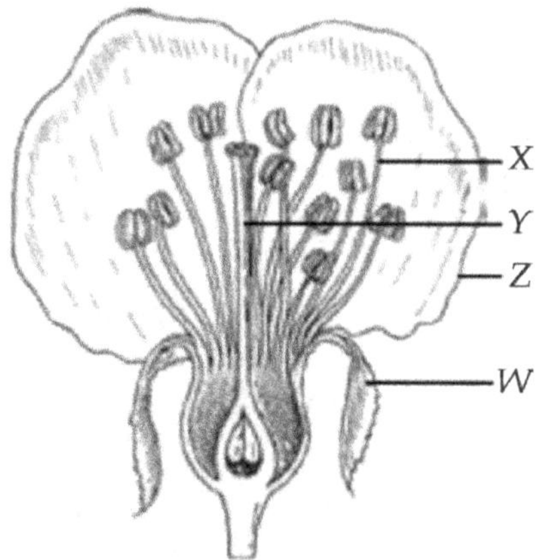

(A) Self pollination is not possible in a flower that lacks either X or Y.

(B) Monoecious plants like maize bear two types of flower, one with X and other with Y.

(C) W and Z constitute non-essential floral whorls.

(D) Plants with flowers having both X and Y can never undergo cross pollination

46. The joints of Latifs garage door are producing sound. To solve this problem, he must apply

(A) Saw dust in the joints of the door

(B) Water in the joints of the door

(C) Sand in the joints of the door

(D) Oil in the joints of the door

47. In a cycling race, it is observed that a cyclist normally bends his body forward (as shown in the given figure).

The cyclist bends in order to
(A) Feel comfortable
(B) Reduce his weight
(C) Reduce the air drag
(D) Increase energy consumption

48. The artificial satellites sent into space by India in ascending order of their launching date is
(A) APPLE, EDUSAT, ROHINI, INSAT 4B
(B) EDUSAT, ROHINI, APPLE, INSAT 4B
(C) ROHINI, APPLE, EDUSAT, INSAT 4B
(D) INSAT 4B, EDUSAT, APPLE, ROHINI

49. Animals exhibiting external fertilisation produce a large number of gametes. Pick the appropriate reason from the following
(A) The animals are small in size and want to produce more offsprings.
(B) Food is available in plenty in water.
(C) To ensure better chance of fertilisation.
(D) Water promotes production of large number of gametes.

50. Refer to the given paragraph where few words have been italicised.

Hormones are produced by organs called endocrine glands. These are ductless glands. Very small quantity of different hormones is required by our body. *Adrenaline* is secreted when we are stressed or excited. *Liver* regulates the sugar metabolism in the body by its hormone *insulin*. *Pineal* glands secrete calcitonin while *thyroid* glands secrete melatonin.

Select the correct option regarding these.
(A) Insulin should be replaced by aldosterone.
(B) Liver should not be replaced as it is correctly mentioned.
(C) Positions of pineal and thyroid should be interchanged.
(D) Adrenaline should be replaced by progesterone.

Darken Your Choice with HB Pencil

1. Ⓐ Ⓑ Ⓒ Ⓓ	11. Ⓐ Ⓑ Ⓒ Ⓓ	21. Ⓐ Ⓑ Ⓒ Ⓓ	31. Ⓐ Ⓑ Ⓒ Ⓓ	41. Ⓐ Ⓑ Ⓒ Ⓓ
2. Ⓐ Ⓑ Ⓒ Ⓓ	12. Ⓐ Ⓑ Ⓒ Ⓓ	22. Ⓐ Ⓑ Ⓒ Ⓓ	32. Ⓐ Ⓑ Ⓒ Ⓓ	42. Ⓐ Ⓑ Ⓒ Ⓓ
3. Ⓐ Ⓑ Ⓒ Ⓓ	13. Ⓐ Ⓑ Ⓒ Ⓓ	23. Ⓐ Ⓑ Ⓒ Ⓓ	33. Ⓐ Ⓑ Ⓒ Ⓓ	43. Ⓐ Ⓑ Ⓒ Ⓓ
4. Ⓐ Ⓑ Ⓒ Ⓓ	14. Ⓐ Ⓑ Ⓒ Ⓓ	24. Ⓐ Ⓑ Ⓒ Ⓓ	34. Ⓐ Ⓑ Ⓒ Ⓓ	44. Ⓐ Ⓑ Ⓒ Ⓓ
5. Ⓐ Ⓑ Ⓒ Ⓓ	15. Ⓐ Ⓑ Ⓒ Ⓓ	25. Ⓐ Ⓑ Ⓒ Ⓓ	35. Ⓐ Ⓑ Ⓒ Ⓓ	45. Ⓐ Ⓑ Ⓒ Ⓓ
6. Ⓐ Ⓑ Ⓒ Ⓓ	16. Ⓐ Ⓑ Ⓒ Ⓓ	26. Ⓐ Ⓑ Ⓒ Ⓓ	36. Ⓐ Ⓑ Ⓒ Ⓓ	46. Ⓐ Ⓑ Ⓒ Ⓓ
7. Ⓐ Ⓑ Ⓒ Ⓓ	17. Ⓐ Ⓑ Ⓒ Ⓓ	27. Ⓐ Ⓑ Ⓒ Ⓓ	37. Ⓐ Ⓑ Ⓒ Ⓓ	47. Ⓐ Ⓑ Ⓒ Ⓓ
8. Ⓐ Ⓑ Ⓒ Ⓓ	18. Ⓐ Ⓑ Ⓒ Ⓓ	28. Ⓐ Ⓑ Ⓒ Ⓓ	38. Ⓐ Ⓑ Ⓒ Ⓓ	48. Ⓐ Ⓑ Ⓒ Ⓓ
9. Ⓐ Ⓑ Ⓒ Ⓓ	19. Ⓐ Ⓑ Ⓒ Ⓓ	29. Ⓐ Ⓑ Ⓒ Ⓓ	39. Ⓐ Ⓑ Ⓒ Ⓓ	49. Ⓐ Ⓑ Ⓒ Ⓓ
10. Ⓐ Ⓑ Ⓒ Ⓓ	20. Ⓐ Ⓑ Ⓒ Ⓓ	30. Ⓐ Ⓑ Ⓒ Ⓓ	40. Ⓐ Ⓑ Ⓒ Ⓓ	50. Ⓐ Ⓑ Ⓒ Ⓓ

1. CROP PRODUCTION AND MANAGEMENT

Answer Key

1. (C)	2. (A)	3. (B)	4. (D)	5. (C)	6. (A)	7. (B)	8. (D)	9. (D)	10. (B)
11. (B)	12. (A)	13. (C)	14. (B)	15. (A)	16. (B)	17. (C)	18. (A)	19. (B)	20. (D)
21. (D)	22. (A)	23. (B)	24. (C)	25. (B)					

HOTS (ACHIEVERS SECTION)

26. (A)	27. (B)	28. (A)	29. (C)	30. (C)

2. MICROORGANISMS

Answer Key

1. (D)	2. (B)	3. (A)	4. (C)	5. (D)	6. (C)	7. (C)	8. (A)	9. (C)	10. (B)
11. (A)	12. (D)	13. (C)	14. (D)	15. (A)	16. (C)	17. (D)	18. (B)	19. (C)	20. (D)
21. (A)	22. (C)	23. (B)	24. (C)	25. (D)					

HOTS (ACHIEVERS SECTION)

26. (A)	27. (B)	28. (D)	29. (A)	30. (A)

3. SYNTHETIC FIBRES AND PLASTICS

Answer Key

1. (B)	2. (B)	3. (A)	4. (C)	5. (A)	6. (D)	7. (C)	8. (B)	9. (B)	10. (C)
11. (D)	12. (D)	13. (A)	14. (A)	15. (B)	16. (D)	17. (A)	18. (C)	19. (A)	20. (C)
21. (B)	22. (A)	23. (B)	24. (B)	25. (C)					

HOTS (ACHIEVERS SECTION)

26. (D)	27. (D)	28. (B)	29. (D)	30. (B)

4. METALS AND NON-METALS

Answer Key

1. (B)	2. (A)	3. (B)	4. (C)	5. (B)	6. (D)	7. (A)	8. (C)	9. (D)	10. (B)
11. (A)	12. (B)	13. (B)	14. (A)	15. (B)	16. (C)	17. (D)	18. (C)	19. (A)	20. (B)
21. (C)	22. (D)	23. (B)	24. (A)	25. (C)	26. (B)	27. (A)	28. (A)	29. (B)	30. (C)

HOTS (ACHIEVERS SECTION)

31. (D)	32. (B)	33. (A)	34. (A)	35. (C)

5. COAL AND PETROLEUM

Answer Key

1. (B)	2. (C)	3. (D)	4. (A)	5. (D)	6. (C)	7. (B)	8. (D)	9. (A)	10. (D)
11. (B)	12. (C)	13. (A)	14. (B)	15. (A)	16. (B)	17. (B)	18. (D)	19. (D)	20. (D)
21. (B)	22. (C)	23. (D)	24. (B)	25. (B)					

HOTS (ACHIEVERS SECTION)

26. (C)	27. (D)	28. (A)	29. (C)	30. (D)

27. (D)
Liquid ammonia, liquid hydrogen and alcohol are suitable as rocket fuels.

28. (A)
Energy released = $12 \times 50KJ = 600KJ$
Therefore, Energy consumed per day
$= \dfrac{600}{30}KJ = 20,000J/day$

6. COMBUSTION AND FLAME

Answer Key

1. (C)	2. (B)	3. (A)	4. (C)	5. (B)	6. (D)	7. (C)	8. (A)	9. (A)	10. (A)
11. (B)	12. (B)	13. (D)	14. (C)	15. (B)	16. (A)	17. (B)	18. (D)	19. (C)	20. (B)
21. (B)	22. (D)	23. (A)	24. (B)	25. (A)					

HOTS (ACHIEVERS SECTION)

26. (B)	27. (D)	28. (C)	29. (B)	30. (C)

26. (B)

Phosphorous applied on the head of a match stick has a very low ignition temperature of 35°C. During rubbing, the heat produced due to friction is sufficient to attain this temperature resulting in combustion.

27. (D)

Lead compound are highly toxic in nature and can cause numerous ailments in human beings and animals. They are absorbed by soil and find their way in food chain.

28. (C)

When coal is burnt in sufficient quantity in big factories, it leaves 10% to 20% of ash. This ash is carried upward due to air and causes pollution problems.

7. CONSERVATION OF PLANTS AND ANIMALS

Answer Key

1. (C)	2. (A)	3. (C)	4. (A)	5. (C)	6. (D)	7. (D)	8. (B)	9. (C)	10. (A)
11. (D)	12. (A)	13. (B)	14. (A)	15. (A)	16. (C)	17. (B)	18. (A)	19. (A)	20. (B)
21. (D)	22. (D)	23. (B)	24. (D)	25. (D)	26. (D)	27. (B)	28. (C)	29. (B)	30. (C)

HOTS (ACHIEVERS SECTION)

31. (B)	32. (D)	33. (A)	34. (A)	35. (A)

8. CELL-STRUCTURE AND FUNCTIONS

Answer Key

1. (B)	2. (A)	3. (D)	4. (D)	5. (C)	6. (B)	7. (C)	8. (D)	9. (A)	10. (C)
11. (A)	12. (B)	13. (B)	14. (B)	15. (D)	16. (B)	17. (A)	18. (B)	19. (C)	20. (A)
21. (A)	22. (A)	23. (C)	24. (B)	25. (A)	26. (D)	27. (D)	28. (A)	29. (B)	30. (B)

HOTS (ACHIEVERS SECTION)

31. (C)	32. (A)	33. (A)	34. (A)	35. (A)

1. (C)

Lysosomes are called digestive organs of the cell which are capable of engulfing of food materials and other substances. These are hydrolysed inside lysosomes by certain enzymes.

9. REPRODUCTION IN ANIMALS

Answer Key

1. (C)	2. (A)	3. (C)	4. (A)	5. (D)	6. (B)	7. (A)	8. (C)	9. (D)	10. (B)
11. (A)	12. (C)	13. (B)	14. (C)	15. (B)	16. (C)	17. (A)	18. (C)	19. (A)	20. (D)
21. (B)	22. (C)	23. (B)	24. (A)	25. (B)	26. (D)	27. (D)	28. (C)	29. (C)	30. (B)

HOTS (ACHIEVERS SECTION)

31. (B)	32. (C)	33. (D)	34. (B)	35. (C)

10. FORCE AND PRESSURE

Answer Key

1. (B)	2. (B)	3. (D)	4. (A)	5. (D)	6. (B)	7. (A)	8. (D)	9. (C)	10 (A)
11. (C)	12. (D)	13. (B)	14. (C)	15. (D)	16. (C)	17. (C)	18. (A)	19. (C)	20. (A)
21. (D)	22. (C)	23. (A)	24. (D)	25. (B)					

HOTS (ACHIEVERS SECTION)

26. (D)	27. (D)	28. (B)	29. (C)	30. (A)

30. (A)

$$\text{Pressure} = \text{Force}/\text{Area} = \frac{20\text{N}}{(4\times10^{-2})\times(4\times10^{-2})\text{m}^2} = 1.25 \times 104 \text{ Pa} = 12{,}500 \text{ Pascal}$$

11. FRICTION

Answer Key

1. (A)	2. (C)	3. (B)	4. (A)	5. (D)	6. (B)	7. (B)	8. (A)	9 (B)	10. (A)
11. (A)	12. (D)	13. (D)	14. (C)	15. (A)	16. (B)	17. (C)	18. (B)	19. (A)	20. (C)
21. (C)	22. (C)	23. (D)	24. (B)	25. (C)					

HOTS (ACHIEVERS SECTION)

26. (A)	27. (A)	28. (D)	29. (C)	30. (D)

Answer Key

1. (A)	2. (C)	3. (B)	4. (D)	5. (A)	6. (B)	7. (C)	8. (C)	9. (D)	10. (D)
11. (A)	12. (B)	13. (D)	14. (A)	15. (B)	16. (C)	17. (B)	18. (C)	19. (C)	20. (B)
21. (D)	22. (B)	23. (A)	24. (B)	25. (A)					

HOTS (ACHIEVERS SECTION)

26. (A)	27. (C)	28. (A)	29. (A)	30. (C)

29. (A)

In a wave motion (like sound wave), the particles of the medium do not travel. It is the disturbance (energy) which travels along the path.

30. (C)

Two vocal chords, stretched across the larynx in such a way that it leaves a narrow slit between them for passage of air. The length of vocal chords and the width of the slit is different in man, woman and child, thus producing different sounds.

13. CHEMICAL EFFECTS OF ELECTRIC CURRENT

Answer Key

1. (D)	2. (A)	3. (C)	4. (C)	5. (B)	6. (D)	7. (C)	8. (D)	9. (C)	10. (C)
11. (A)	12. (B)	13. (A)	14. (C)	15. (D)	16. (D)	17. (B)	18. (A)	19. (B)	20. (A)
21. (C)	22. (C)	23. (B)	24. (A)	25. (C)					

HOTS (ACHIEVERS SECTION)

26. (D)	27. (D)	28. (B)	29. (C)	30. (A)

27. (D)

Due to the heating effect of current, the filament of the bulb gets heated to a high temperature and it starts glowing.

28. (B)

In cells, electrons move from negative electrode to positive electrode as an electron has a negative charge. However by convention, flow of charges are measured only through positive charges. When an electron moves from point A to B, an equal amount of positive charge moves from point B to A. So, the direction of charge is from positive electrode to negative electrode.

Answer Key

1. (B)	2. (C)	3. (A)	4. (D)	5. (B)	6. (D)	7. (D)	8. (C)	9. (A)	10. (D)
11. (D)	12. (D)	13. (B)	14. (D)	15. (C)	16. (A)	17. (C)	18. (C)	19. (D)	20. (B)
21. (A)	22. (C)	23. (C)	24. (A)	25. (B)	26. (D)	27. (B)	28. (B)	29. (C)	30. (A)

HOTS (ACHIEVERS SECTION)

31. (B)	32. (C)	33. (D)	34. (D)	35. (A)

31. (B)
The accumulated charges on clouds pass through air which is a poor conductor of electricity. When the negative and positive charges meet, they produce streaks of bright light.

32. (C)
Squatting low on ground will make you the smallest target to be struck. In all other cases, you are exposed to the atmosphere.

33. (D)
SO_2 gas released during the burning of coal and oxides of nitrogen released during combustion of petrol dissolve in rain water and form rain acids.

15. LIGHT

Answer Key

1. (B)	2. (C)	3. (A)	4. (D)	5. (C)	6. (B)	7. (A)	8. (B)	9. (C)	10. (B)
11. (A)	12. (C)	13. (D)	14. (C)	15. (B)	16. (A)	17. (D)	18. (C)	19. (B)	20. (C)
21. (D)	22. (A)	23. (C)	24. (B)	25. (A)					

HOTS (ACHIEVERS SECTION)

26. (D)	27. (D)	28. (A)	29. (C)	30. (D)

28. (A)
It is a phenomenon where the brain continues to sense the image even after the object has been removed. This lasts for 1/16th of a second.

29. (C)
The dots are arranged in cells of two vertical rows of three dots each to form 63 characters.

30. (D)
The nocturnal animals need more light to see at night the large cornea and pupil allow more light into their eyes.

16. STARS AND THE SOLAR SYSTEM

Answer Key

1. (C)	2. (D)	3. (C)	4. (B)	5. (A)	6. (D)	7 (C)	8. (D)	9. (B)	10. (C)
11. (A)	12. (D)	13. (B)	14. (C)	15. (A)	16. (B)	17. (C)	18. (A)	19. (D)	20. (A)
21. (C)	22. (C)	23. (B)	24. (B)	25. (D)					

HOTS (ACHIEVERS SECTION)

26. (D)	27. (B)	28. (C)	29. (B)	30. (A)

17. POLLUTION OF AIR AND WATER

Answer Key

1. (D)	2. (C)	3. (D)	4. (B)	5. (A)	6. (C)	7. (D)	8. (C)	9. (B)	10. (C)
11. (D)	12. (D)	13. (A)	14. (C)	15. (B)	16. (B)	17. (D)	18. (C)	19. (D)	20. (B)
21. (A)	22. (C)	23. (B)	24. (A)	25. (B)	26. (D)	27. (D)	28. (A)	29. (A)	30. (C)

HOTS (ACHIEVERS SECTION)

31. (C)	32. (A)	33. (B)	34. (C)	35. (A)

18. LOGICAL REASONING

Answer Key

1. (C)	2. (D)	3. (C)	4. (B)	5. (A)	6. (A)	7. (D)	8. (B)	9. (A)	10. (B)
11. (A)	12. (B)	13. (B)	14. (B)	15. (A)	16. (B)	17. (C)	18. (A)	19. (B)	20. (A)
21. (A)	22. (C)	23. (B)	24. (C)	25. (B)	26. (C)	27. (A)	28. (B)	29. (B)	30. (B)
31. (C)	32. (A)	33. (A)	34. (B)	35. (B)	36. (C)	37. (D)	38. (B)	39. (C)	40. (A)
41. (A)	42. (C)	43. (D)	44. (C)	45. (C)	46. (A)	47. (D)	48. (A)	49. (D)	50. (D)
51. (A)	52. (D)	53. (C)	54. (A)	55. (C)	56. (A)	57. (B)	58. (B)	59. (D)	60. (D)
61. (A)	62. (D)	63. (A)	64. (D)	65. (D)					

1. **(C)**
   Z = 26; O = 15
   ZOO = 26 + 15 + 15 = 56
   D = 4, E = 5; R = 18
   DEER = 4 + 5 + 5 + 18 = 32
   LION = 12 + 9 + 15 + 14 = 50

2. **(D)**
   JEANS = 10 + 5 + 1 + 14 + 19 = 49
   COAT = 3 + 15 + 1 + 20 = 39
   SHIRT = 19 + 8 + 9 + 18 + 20 = 74

3. **(C)**
   BUD = 2 + 21 + 4 = 27
   ROSE = 18 + 15 + 19 + 5 = 57
   FLOWER = 6 + 12 + 15 + 23 + 5 + 18 = 79

4. **(B)**
   BMX, DNW, FOU, HPT

5. **(A)**
   UPI, SHJ, ODP, MBQ, IAW

6. **(A)**
   Spanner is used by carpenter and all other tools are used by gardener.

7. **(D)**
   All except oasis are related to sea.

8. **(B)**
   All except Appendix are bones of our body.

9. **(A)**
   Siachen is a glacier, but all other are lakes.

10. **(B)**
    All except Physics are branch of Physics.

11. **(A)**
    In this code, a letter is the nth letter from the beginning of English alphabet then in the code the corresponding letter is the nth letter from the end.
    $$\text{HAND} \rightarrow \text{SZMW}$$
    then MILK $\rightarrow$ NROP

12. **(B)**

    T U R N
    (+2↓ +2↓ +2↓ +2↓)
    V W T P

    Similarly   W A L K
    (+2↓ +2↓ +2↓ +2↓)
    Y C N M

13. **(B)**

    G U A V A
    (+1↓ +1↓ +1↓ +1↓ +1↓)
    H V B W B

    Similarly   J U I C E
    (+1↓ +1↓ +1↓ +1↓ +1↓)
    K V J D F

14. **(B)**

    J U M P
    (−1↓ −1↓ −1↓ −1↓)
    I T L O

    Similarly   R O U N D
    (−1↓ −1↓ −1↓ −1↓ −1↓)
    Q N T M C

15. **(A)**
    Position of letters in English alphabet
    AT = 1 + 20 = 21.
    CAT = 3 + 1 + 20 = 24
    MAT = 13 + 1 + 20 = 34

16. **(B)**
    Starting position of Nitesh is A and his final position is F which is in the South-East direction from starting point.

    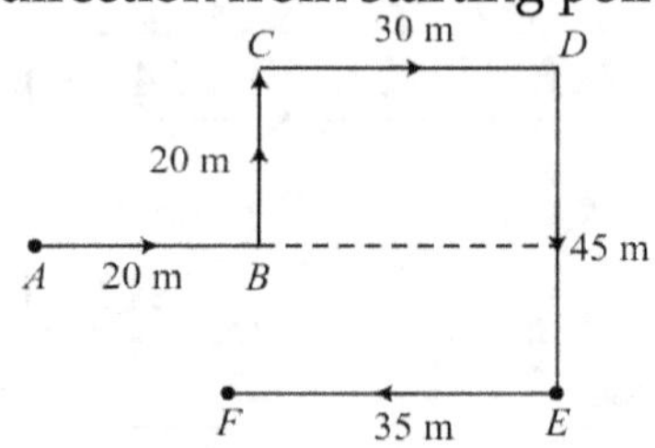

17. **(C)**

    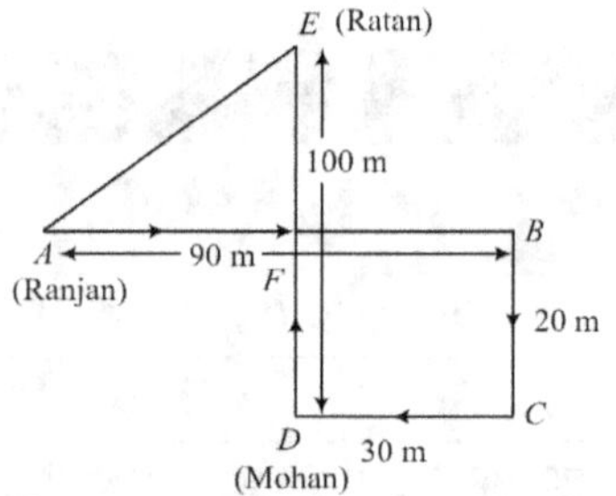

    In the above Fig. A is Ranjan's position and E is Ratan's position. The required distance = AE

    $$AE = \sqrt{(AF)^2 + EF^2}$$
    $$= \sqrt{(90-30)^2 + (100-20)^2}$$

$$= \sqrt{3600 + 6400} = 100 \text{ m}$$

18. (A)

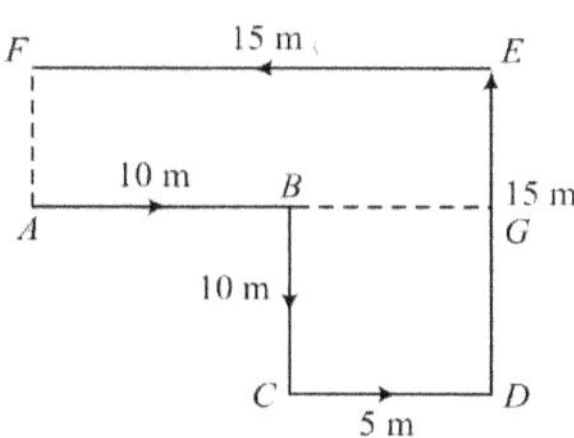

Dinesh starts from A his final position is at F.

AF = DE – GD = 15 – 10 = 5 m

19. (B)

Pritam's starting point is at A.

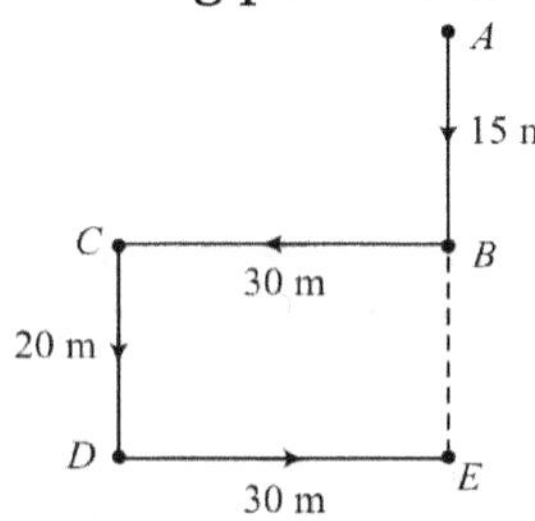

Final position is E.

$$AE = AB + BE$$
$$= AB + CD$$
$$= 15 + 20$$
$$= 35 \text{ m}$$

20. (A)

Ankit's final position is OC, which is in North-East.

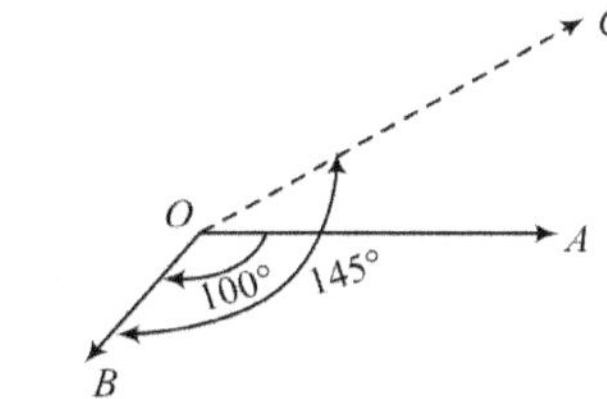

21. (A)

6   15   28   45   66   91

+ 9   + 13   + 17   + 21   + 25

22. (C)

12   19   28   39   52   67

+ 7   + 9   + 11   + 13   + 15

23. (B)

10   22   46   94   190

+ 12   + 24   + 48   + 96

24. (C)

15   31   63   127   255   511

× 2 + 1   × 2 + 1   × 2 + 1   × 2 + 1   × 2 + 1

25. (B)

40320   5760   960   192   48   16

÷ 7   ÷ 6   ÷ 5   ÷ 4   ÷ 3

26. (C)

$$(5 + 6 + 7) \times 3 = 18 \times 3 = 54$$
$$(7 + 11 + 8) \times 3 = 26 \times 3 = 78$$
$$\therefore ? = (8 + 12 + 9) \times 3 = 29 \times 3 = 87$$

27. (A)

$$\frac{134 - 102}{4} = \frac{32}{4} = 8$$

$$\frac{227 - 143}{4} = \frac{84}{4} = 21$$

$$\therefore ? = \frac{198 - 154}{4} = \frac{44}{4} = 11$$

28. (B)

$$4^2 + 5^2 = 16 + 25 = 41$$
$$12^2 + 8^2 = 144 + 64 = 208$$
$$\Rightarrow 24^2 + x^2 = 832$$
$$\Rightarrow x^2 = 832 - 576 = 256$$
$$\Rightarrow x = 16$$

29. (B)

$$(18 - 7)^2 = 11^2 = 121$$
$$(21 - 8)^2 = 13^2 = 169$$
$$\therefore ? = (25 - 13)^2 = 12^2 = 144$$

30. (B)

$$(25)^2 - (18)^2 = 625 - 324 = 301$$
$$(27)^2 - (16)^2 = 729 - 256 = 473$$
$$\therefore ? = (23)^2 - (9)^2 = 529 - 81 = 448$$

31. (C)

5 1   4 7 3   9 8   5 7 2   6 3 1   5 8 6 3 8 5 2 2 4 3 4 9 6

32. (A)

5 1 4 7 3 2 5 6 8 9 6 7 3 2 1 5 6 4 3 2 7 4

33. (A)

8 4 7 6 5 3 2 5 1 6 4 3 2 6 7 9 8 5

34. (B)

2 5 3 4 8 7 4 2 6 7 1 5 8 3 7 4 5 3

35. (B)

2 3 4 5 6 1 4 5 7 1 2 4 5 7 3 8 4 5 9 6 5 3

36. (C)

$12 + 8 + 4 + 4 = 28$

37. (D)

$8 + 10 + 5 + 2 + 1 + 1 = 27$

38. (B)

$6 + 6 + 2 + 1 = 15$

39. (C)

$10 + 2 + 4 + 2 = 18$

40. (A)

$16 + 4 + 8 + 4 + 4 + 8 + 4 = 48$

61. (D)

There are there types of faces, hands and legs. Each type is used once in each row.

62. (A)

The 2nd figure is obtained from the first figure by reversing the direction of RHS arrow. and 3rd figure is obtained from second figure by reversing the direction of each arrow.

MODEL TEST PAPER

Answer Key

1. (B)	2. (C)	3. (D)	4. (C)	5. (C)	6. (A)	7. (D)	8. (D)	9. (C)	10. (D)
11. (A)	12. (A)	13. (D)	14. (C)	15. (C)	16. (A)	17. (C)	18. (C)	19. (A)	20. (D)
21. (C)	22. (B)	23. (B)	24. (C)	25. (B)	26. (D)	27. (B)	28. (B)	29. (C)	30. (A)
31. (C)	32. (D)	33. (D)	34. (B)	35. (C)	36. (B)	37. (D)	38. (B)	39. (B)	40. (A)
41. (A)	42. (A)	43. (A)	44. (D)	45. (D)	46. (D)	47. (C)	48. (C)	49. (C)	50. (C)

SAMPLE OMR ANSWER SHEET

1. STUDENT NAME (IN ENGLISH CAPITAL LETTERS ONLY)

Students must write and darken the respective circles completely using HB Pencil only. Othewise their Answer Sheets will not be evaluated.

PERSONAL DETAILS

2. SCHOOL CODE

3. CLASS

4. SECTION

5. ROLL NO.

6. QUESTION PAPER SET

A ○
B ○
C ○
D ○

7. MOBILE NUMBER

8. GENDER

MALE ○
FEMALE ○

9. STREAM
(Only for Class XI and XII Students)

MATHEMATICS ○
BIOLOGY ○
OTHERS ○

MARK YOUR ANSWERS

No.	A	B	C	D	No.	A	B	C	D
1.	Ⓐ	Ⓑ	Ⓒ	Ⓓ	26.	Ⓐ	Ⓑ	Ⓒ	Ⓓ
2.	Ⓐ	Ⓑ	Ⓒ	Ⓓ	27.	Ⓐ	Ⓑ	Ⓒ	Ⓓ
3.	Ⓐ	Ⓑ	Ⓒ	Ⓓ	28.	Ⓐ	Ⓑ	Ⓒ	Ⓓ
4.	Ⓐ	Ⓑ	Ⓒ	Ⓓ	29.	Ⓐ	Ⓑ	Ⓒ	Ⓓ
5.	Ⓐ	Ⓑ	Ⓒ	Ⓓ	30.	Ⓐ	Ⓑ	Ⓒ	Ⓓ
6.	Ⓐ	Ⓑ	Ⓒ	Ⓓ	31.	Ⓐ	Ⓑ	Ⓒ	Ⓓ
7.	Ⓐ	Ⓑ	Ⓒ	Ⓓ	32.	Ⓐ	Ⓑ	Ⓒ	Ⓓ
8.	Ⓐ	Ⓑ	Ⓒ	Ⓓ	33.	Ⓐ	Ⓑ	Ⓒ	Ⓓ
9.	Ⓐ	Ⓑ	Ⓒ	Ⓓ	34.	Ⓐ	Ⓑ	Ⓒ	Ⓓ
10.	Ⓐ	Ⓑ	Ⓒ	Ⓓ	35.	Ⓐ	Ⓑ	Ⓒ	Ⓓ
11.	Ⓐ	Ⓑ	Ⓒ	Ⓓ	36.	Ⓐ	Ⓑ	Ⓒ	Ⓓ
12.	Ⓐ	Ⓑ	Ⓒ	Ⓓ	37.	Ⓐ	Ⓑ	Ⓒ	Ⓓ
13.	Ⓐ	Ⓑ	Ⓒ	Ⓓ	38.	Ⓐ	Ⓑ	Ⓒ	Ⓓ
14.	Ⓐ	Ⓑ	Ⓒ	Ⓓ	39.	Ⓐ	Ⓑ	Ⓒ	Ⓓ
15.	Ⓐ	Ⓑ	Ⓒ	Ⓓ	40.	Ⓐ	Ⓑ	Ⓒ	Ⓓ
16.	Ⓐ	Ⓑ	Ⓒ	Ⓓ	41.	Ⓐ	Ⓑ	Ⓒ	Ⓓ
17.	Ⓐ	Ⓑ	Ⓒ	Ⓓ	42.	Ⓐ	Ⓑ	Ⓒ	Ⓓ
18.	Ⓐ	Ⓑ	Ⓒ	Ⓓ	43.	Ⓐ	Ⓑ	Ⓒ	Ⓓ
19.	Ⓐ	Ⓑ	Ⓒ	Ⓓ	44.	Ⓐ	Ⓑ	Ⓒ	Ⓓ
20.	Ⓐ	Ⓑ	Ⓒ	Ⓓ	45.	Ⓐ	Ⓑ	Ⓒ	Ⓓ
21.	Ⓐ	Ⓑ	Ⓒ	Ⓓ	46.	Ⓐ	Ⓑ	Ⓒ	Ⓓ
22.	Ⓐ	Ⓑ	Ⓒ	Ⓓ	47.	Ⓐ	Ⓑ	Ⓒ	Ⓓ
23.	Ⓐ	Ⓑ	Ⓒ	Ⓓ	48.	Ⓐ	Ⓑ	Ⓒ	Ⓓ
24.	Ⓐ	Ⓑ	Ⓒ	Ⓓ	49.	Ⓐ	Ⓑ	Ⓒ	Ⓓ
25.	Ⓐ	Ⓑ	Ⓒ	Ⓓ	50.	Ⓐ	Ⓑ	Ⓒ	Ⓓ

Signature of the Student & Date of Examination

Signature of the Invigilator & Date of Examination